11

REVISION

Tax Planning

Sue Short

Published by Certified Accountants Educational Projects Ltd

Subject consultant
David Harrowven

Sections 1, 3, 4 and 8
Cathy Lake, Ruth Turley

Commissioning editor
Jane Elliot

Managing editor
Eileen Cadman

Copy editor
Rick Bouwman

Proofreader
James Ryan

Production
Frances Follin, Petra Green

DTP
Goodfellow & Egan

Design
Carla Turchini

Cover design
Fielding Rowinski

Acknowledgements
Past exam questions and articles from the *Students' Newsletter* are reproduced with the kind permission of the Chartered Association of Certified Accountants.

First edition published March 1994
Second edition published August 1994

Certified Accountants Educational Projects Limited
29 Lincoln's Inn Fields
London WC2A 3EE

ISBN 1 85908 091 X

Further information on Certified Accountants Educational Projects Limited products and services may be obtained from Certified Accountants Educational Projects Limited, 29 Lincoln's Inn Fields, London WC2A 3EE.

British Library Cataloguing in Publication data.
A catalogue record for this book is available from the British Library.

Printed by Staples Printers, St Albans

CONTENTS

1 **INTRODUCTION** 1

How to use this revision text
Examinable legislation
Format of the examination paper
The syllabus for Paper 11

2 **REFERENCE TABLE** 7

3 **GENERAL REVISION GUIDANCE** 10

Planning your revision

4 **EXAMINATION TECHNIQUES** 15

The examination

5 **KEY REVISION TOPICS** 20

6 **ANALYSIS OF PAST PAPERS** 31

7 **STUDENTS' NEWSLETTER ARTICLES** 32

8 **UPDATES** 40

Guidance notes

9 **EXAM STYLE QUESTIONS** 45

10 **PILOT PAPER QUESTIONS** 68

11 **MOCK EXAMINATION** 75

12 **ANSWERS TO EXAM STYLE QUESTIONS** 81

13 **ANSWERS TO PILOT PAPER QUESTIONS** 122

14 **ANSWERS TO MOCK EXAMINATION** 132

SECTION 1

INTRODUCTION

How to use this revision text

The aim of this book is to help you maximise the effect of the work you do in the few vital weeks before the examination. It brings together information about the syllabus and the examination paper, general advice on revision and examination techniques, a bank of examination style questions and mock examination paper.

This is a revision text, not a course book. It should be used in conjunction with the textbook or workbooks with which you have studied the full content of the syllabus.

There are many ways of using this book. It has been designed to be as versatile as possible. You may choose to go through it from cover to cover, or to select only those elements which are of particular use to you in your revision. This is what the various sections of the book have to offer:

Section 1 Introduction

This is primarily a reference section. It contains the full syllabus, notes on examinable material for the November 1994 diet and a description of the format of the examination paper. *The information contained in this section is correct at 31 December 1993. The* Students' Newsletter *will contain any subsequent changes to the exam or the syllabus.*

Section 2 Reference table

This section links the examination style questions in Section 9 with the syllabus. You can use it to plan the order in which to revise syllabus topics, or to select the questions which you will work through. The section also contains a table which you can use to locate coverage of syllabus topics in the textbooks and open learning workbooks published by ACCA.

Section 3 General revision guidance

This section offers suggestions on how you can plan your general revision strategy. You may find it useful to read it before you embark on detailed revision.

Section 4 Examination techniques

Practical advice about the examination is accompanied by some suggestions on how to tackle the kinds of questions you are likely to meet in this paper.

Section 5 Key revision topics

This is a checklist of key information. You may use it to provide the structure of your revision plan, or as a quick reminder of the topics you should have covered.

1

Section 6 Analysis of past papers

As the June 1994 examination will be the first paper for the new ACCA syllabus, general advice only can be given in this section.

Section 7 *Students' Newsletter* articles

This brings together relevant articles which have appeared in the *Students' Newsletter* or elsewhere.

Section 8 Updates

This section includes detailed guidance from the Examiner on the syllabus. It is based on the annual meetings held for teachers at ACCA. *The information contained in this section is correct at 31 December 1993. The* Students' Newsletter *will contain any subsequent changes to the exam or the syllabus.*

Section 9 Exam style questions

This selection of questions is designed to give representative coverage of the syllabus. This section is perhaps the most important part of the book and we suggest that you work through as many of the questions as possible.

Section 10 Pilot paper questions

These questions illustrate the style and format of the examination. They also provide further opportunities for practice.

Section 11 Mock examination

We suggest that you work through this paper under exam conditions. You will probably get most out of it if you attempt it at a fairly late stage in your revision.

Section 12 Answers to exam style questions

These answers are annotated to indicate where marks can be gained or lost. You should not refer to them until you have attempted the questions in Section 9.

Section 13 Answers to pilot paper questions

Once again, you should not refer to these answers until you have worked through the questions.

Section 14 Answers to mock examination

These answers will enable you to judge how well you fared in the mock examination.

Examinable legislation

The ACCA applies a six-month rule in that questions requiring an understanding of new legislation will not be set out until at least six calendar months after the last day of the month in which the legislation received Royal Assent or similar procedure in any of the other countries. The same rule applies to the effective date of the provisions of an Act introduced by Statutory Instrument.

1

The Finance Acts

The latest Finance Act which will be examined at the December 1994 session is the Finance Act 1994 (FA94) and you are advised to use text(s) which reflect the FA94 for your preparation for the exam.

With regard to prospective legislation when, for example, provisions included in the Finance Act will only take effect at some date in the future, such legislation will not normally be examined until such time as it actually takes effect.

Tax rates and allowances

The following tax rates and allowances will always be reproduced in the exam. In addition, other specific extracts and information necessary for candidates to answer questions set will be given as required. For example, in the case of capital gains tax, the retail prices index for particular dates and extracts from the lease percentages tables will be given.

Income tax

		%
Lower rate	£1 – £3,000	20
Basic rate	£3,001 – £23,700	25
Higher rate	£23,701 and above	40

Personal allowances

	£
Personal allowance	3,445
Personal allowance – 65–74	4,200
Personal allowance – 75 and over	4,370
Married couple's allowance	1,720 *
Married couple's allowance – 65–74	2,665 *
Married couple's allowance – 75 and over	2,705 *
Income limit for age-related allowances	14,200
Additional personal allowance	1,720 *
Widow's bereavement allowance	1,720 *
Blind person's allowance	1,080

*Allowances where relief is restricted to 20%. (The exam does not highlight this.)

Car benefit tables

	Fuel	
	Petrol	Diesel
	£	£
1,400cc or less	640	580
1,401cc to 2,000cc	810	580
2,001cc and over	1,200	750

1

Mobile telephone

Cash equivalent of benefit	£200

Personal pension contribution limits

Age	Maximum percentage %
Up to 35	17.5
36 – 45	20
46 – 50	25
51 – 55	30
56 – 60	35
61 or more	40

(Earnings cap £76,800)

Capital allowances

	%
Plant and machinery	
Writing down allowance	25
Industrial buildings allowance	
Writing down allowance	4
Agricultural buildings allowance	
Writing down allowance	4

Corporation tax

Financial year	Full rate	Small Companies rate	Taper Relief fraction	Act fraction	Upper limit	Lower limit
1988	35	25	1/40	25/75	500,000	100,000
1989	35	25	1/40	25/75	750,000	150,000
1990	34	25	9/400	25/75	1,000,000	200,000
1991	33	25	1/50	25/75	1,250,000	250,000
1992	33	25	1/50	25/75	1,250,000	250,000
1993	33	25	1/50	22.5/77.5	1,250,000	250,000
1994	33	25	1/50	20/80	1,500,000	300,000

Marginal relief

$(M - P) \times I/P \times$ Tapering relief fraction

Inheritance tax

£1 – £150,000	Nil
Excess	40%

Rates of interest

'Official rate' of interest: 10% (assumed)
Rates of interest on underpaid/overpaid tax: 10% (assumed)

Capital gains tax

Lease percentage table: The relevant extracts from this table will be given as appropriate.
Annual exemption: individuals £5,800
Retail price index: The relevant indices will be given as appropriate.

National insurance (not contracted out rates)

		Rate		Lower limit	Upper limit
				£	£
Class 1	Employee	10%	1	57 p.w.	430 p.w.
	Employer	10.2%	2	57 p.w.	–
Class 2		£5.65 per week			
Class 4		7.3%		6,490 p.a.	22,360 p.a.

1 Earnings below £57 per week are exempt; where earnings exceed this limit the first £57 per week is taxable at a reduced rate of 2%.

2 Reduced rates apply in respect of low earnings, as follows:

Band		
£	£	%
57 –	99.99	3.6
100 –	144.99	5.6
145 –	199.99	7.6

Format of the examination paper

	Number of marks
4 (out of 6) questions of 25 marks each	100

You are reminded that the questions for this and subsequent papers will normally focus on everyday situations and accordingly, it will be relatively unusual for a question to involve knowledge of only one tax. While there will generally be some computational elements in each question, long and involved calculations will not be called for. The emphasis will rather be on your appreciation of how the various taxes may impact on a given situation. You will also be expected to appreciate the more common interactions between the taxes and be able to indentify basic tax planning points where appropriate. You will be expected to demonstrate your ability to communicate your findings and recommendations to clients, as well as to explain clearly the more important principles of tax law.

You are advised that a knowledge of section numbers will not be needed to understand questions in this paper, nor will you be expected to use them in your answers. If you wish to refer to section numbers in your answers, you may do so and will not be penalised if old, or even incorrect, section numbers are used.

With regard to the new current year basis of assessment for the self-employed, the change to this basis as from 1997–98, with 1996–97 being the year of transition, is presently not examinable. However, you should be aware that the change is imminent when, for example, providing taxation advice on whether or not to incorporate a business. Although the new basis will apply immediately to new businesses commencing after 5 April 1994, a *detailed computational* question on this area *will not be set* at the December 1994 diet.

With regard to capital gains tax, you should be aware of the statement made by the Treasury that the existing practice as regards roll-over relief for groups will continue, regardless of the final outcome of the case of *Campbell Connelly & Co Ltd* v *Barnett.*

With regard to inheritance tax, you are reminded that the new Inland Revenue practice in respect of the allocation of annual exemptions, where there is both a PET and a chargeable lifetime transfer in the same year, should be used.

1 The syllabus for Paper 11

The syllabus includes everything examinable in Paper 7, Tax Framework, but extends and deepens the coverage. It also includes some new areas. Topics will be examined so that emphasis is given to simple planning to minimise or defer tax; the application of the tax knowledge to problems encountered in practice; and the inter-relationship of taxes.

1 *Overview of personal business taxation*

- *a* *Interactions between different taxes in a range of situations or transactions.*
- *b* *Tax planning: the application of tax planning measures appropriate to the particular situation.*

2 *Capital Gains Tax*

Application of Capital Gains Tax to individuals and corporate tax payers, with emphasis on business situations.

3 *Inheritance Tax*

- *a* *Principles and scope.*
- *b* *Rules basis and application.*
- *c* *Calculating the tax due by clients.*
- *d* *Minimising/deferring tax liabilities by identifying/applying relevant exemptions, reliefs and allowances.*

4 *Trusts*

Application to trusts of Income Tax, Capital Gains Tax and Inheritance Tax.

5 *Value Added Tax*

The application of Value Added Tax to transactions and other activities of corporate taxpayers.

6 *Corporate Taxation*

- *a* *Groups and consortia.*
- *b* *The provisions covering liquidations and areas such as disincorporations, purchases of own shares, sales and acquisitions of subsidiaries, and share-for-share amalgamations.*
- *c* *Implications of a company being classed as an investment or close company.*

7 *Overseas activities giving rise to taxation liabilities*

- *a* *Definition of residence, ordinary residence and domicile.*
- *b* *The taxation of UK income and gains of non-domicile individuals.*
- *c* *Overseas income and gains: the UK tax treatment of overseas income and gains of UK resident individuals and companies, including relief for double taxation.*
- *d* *Overseas persons, the UK tax treatment of income and gains arising within the UK to non-resident individuals and companies.*
- *e* *The Inheritance Tax position regarding overseas assets of UK individuals and UK assets of non-resident individuals.*
- *f* *Business structures, including a UK branch/subsidiary of a foreign company/group and a foreign branch/subsidiary of a UK company/group.*
- *g* *Anti-avoidance legislation relating to overseas activities, income or persons.*

8 *General*

- *a* *Interrelationship of taxes: the effect of any of the taxes in a given situation or on a particular transaction.*
- *b* *Anti-avoidance: appreciation of the main areas of anti-avoidance legislation and of the enquiry and investigation procedures of the Inland Revenue and Customs and Excise.*

9 *Personal finance*

- *a* *Assisting clients in the determination of personal financial objectives, taking into account such factors as individual circumstances, expectations and the economic environment.*
- *b* *Determining financial needs of clients (how much, when, for how long, and for what purpose?).*
- *c* *Regulations affecting investment advisers, and ethical considerations, including the definition of investment business.*
- *d* *Advising on sources and costs of different forms of finance and their applicability to different circumstances including*
  - *i) bank borrowing*
  - *ii) finance houses*
  - *iii) mortgages*
  - *iv) money and capital markets.*
- *e* *Advising on investment of clients' personal funds*
  - *i) insurance policies*
  - *ii) pension funds*
  - *iii) unit and investment trusts*
  - *iv) TESSAs*
  - *v) PEPs*
  - *vi) equity shares*
  - *vii) gilt edged securities and other bonds*
  - *viii) real property*
  - *ix) banks and building societies*
  - *x) national savings.*

REFERENCE TABLE

a table matching the syllabus with the textbooks, open learning and the revision text

This Section contains a table which shows the links between the syllabus for this paper, Paper 7 and this revision text, as well as the relevant chapters from the ACCA textbook and the workbooks in the Open Learning programme. Syllabus references to Paper 7 have been included because a thorough understanding of Paper 7 is essential for the study of Paper 11.

You can use the table to plan the order in which you revise syllabus topics, or to select the questions you will work through.

Syllabus Papers 7 & 11	Textbook chapters	Open learning sections	Revision topics	Pilot paper questions 1	2	3	4	5	6	Mock exam questions 1	2	3	4	5	6
Paper 7	1–7	W1 S1–7, 9–14	1–7			■			■	■	■	■			■
	15–25	W1 S19, W2 S1–4				■			■	■	■	■			■
	15–25	W3 S1–9, W3 S12–17	13–15			■			■	■	■	■			■
		W3 S19–22				■			■	■	■	■			■
		W4 S1–4, 6				■			■	■	■	■			■
Paper 11															
1a	15–22	W3 S1–9	2–5			■				■					■
1b	15–22	W3 S10, 14–17	2–5			■				■					
2	4–7	W1 S9–14	6–7	■		■		■	■	■	■			■	
2	20–21	W3 S14–17, W4 S11	6–7	■		■		■	■	■	■			■	
3a	8–10	W2 S9, 18	8–11		■						■		■		
3b	8–10	W2 S10, 13, 15, 16	8–11		■						■		■		
3c	8–10	W2 S10–11	10		■						■		■		
3d	8–10	W2 S12, 14	8, 9, 11		■	■					■		■		
4	14	W2 S19–21	12		■										
5	22	W3 S19–23	13						■	■		■			
6a	27	W4 S9–11	16–18					■						■	
6b	28	W4 S12						■							
6c	26	W4 S7						■				■			
7a	30	W2 S5					■						■		
7b	30	W2 S6	19												
7c	30–32	W2 S6, W4 S5, 13	19, 20, 21				■	■					■		
7d	30–32	W2 S7, W4 S14	20				■								
7e	30	W2 S16	19										■		
7f	32–33	W4 S13–14	15				■								
7g	30–33	W4 S13					■								
8a	34	W3 S22, W4 S14, W4 S18–21		■		■		■		■	■	■		■	■
8b	29	W1 S20, W3 S22, W4 S6	14, 15				■							■	
9a	11, 13	W1 S17	22	■											■
9b	11, 13	W1 S17	22	■											■
9c	12	W1 S18		■											
9d	11	W4 S17							■						
9e	4, 11	W1 S16–17	22	■											■

Syllabus Papers 7 & 11	Exam style questions																					
	1	2	3	4	5	6	7	8	9	10	11	12	13	14	15	16	17	18	19	20	21	22
Paper 7	■	■	■	■	■	■	■	■	■	■	■	■	■		■	■						■
Paper 11																						
1a	■		■	■	■		■		■													
1b	■		■	■	■		■		■		■											
2	■	■			■		■	■	■		■	■		■		■	■	■	■			
3a								■				■	■	■								
3b								■				■	■	■								
3c								■				■	■	■								
3d								■				■	■	■								
4								■					■	■								
5			■	■	■	■	■			■								■				
6a															■	■	■	■				
6b															■	■		■	■			
6c	■					■												■				
7a																				■	■	
7b																				■		
7c																				■		
7d																					■	
7e																					■	
7f																	■			■		
7g																					■	
8a		■		■	■	■		■				■		■		■	■	■	■			
8b			■																			
9a							■															■
9b							■															■
9c																						■
9d				■		■												■				
9e			■	■			■															■

SECTION

3

GENERAL REVISION GUIDANCE

Planning your revision

What is revision?

Revision is the process by which you remind yourself of the material you have studied during your course, clarify any problem areas and bring your knowledge to a state where you can retrieve it and present it in a way that will satisfy the Examiners.

Revision is not a substitute for hard work earlier in the course. The syllabus for this paper is too large to be hastily 'crammed' a week or so before the examination. You should think of your revision as the final stage in your study of any topic. It can only be effective if you have already completed earlier stages.

Ideally, you should begin your revision shortly after you begin an examination course. At the end of every week and at the end of every month, you should review the topics you have covered. If you constantly consolidate your work and integrate revision into your normal pattern of study, you should find that the final period of revision – and the examination itself – are much less daunting.

If you are reading this revision text while you are still working through your course, we strongly suggest that you begin now to review the earlier work you did for this paper. Remember, the more times you return to a topic, the more confident you will become with it.

The main purpose of this book, however, is to help you to make the best use of the last few weeks before the examination. In this section we offer some suggestions for effective planning of your final revision and discuss some revision techniques which you may find helpful.

Planning your time

Most candidates find themselves in the position where they have less time than they would like to revise, particularly if they are taking several papers at one diet. The majority of people must balance their study with conflicting demands from work, family or other commitments.

It is impossible to give hard and fast rules about the amount of revision you should do. You should aim to start your final revision at least four weeks before your examination. If you finish your course work earlier than this, you would be well advised to take full advantage of the extra time available to you. The number of hours you spend revising each week will depend on many factors, including the number of papers you are sitting. You should probably aim to do a minimum of about six to eight hours a week for each paper.

In order to make best use of the revision time that you have, it is worth spending a little of it at the planning stage. We suggest that you begin by asking yourself two questions:

- ▶ How much time do I have available for revision?
- ▶ What do I need to cover during my revision?

3

Once you have answered these questions, you should be able to draw up a detailed timetable. We will now consider these questions in more detail.

How much time do I have available for revision?

Many people find it helpful to work out a regular weekly pattern for their revision. We suggest you use the time planning chart provided to do this. Your aim should be to construct a timetable that is sustainable over a period of several weeks.

	Monday	Tuesday	Wednesday	Thursday	Friday	Saturday	Sunday
00.00							
01.00							
02.00							
03.00							
04.00							
05.00							
06.00							
07.00							
08.00							
09.00							
10.00							
11.00							
12.00							
13.00							
14.00							
15.00							
16.00							
17.00							
18.00							
19.00							
20.00							
21.00							
22.00							
23.00							

1 First, block out all the time that is **definitely unavailable** for revision. This will include the hours when you normally sleep, the time you are at work and any other regular and clear commitments.

2 Think about **other people's claims on your time**. If you have a family, or friends whom you see regularly, you may want to discuss your plans with them. People are likely to be flexible in the demands they make on you in the run-up to your examinations, especially if they are aware that you have considered their needs as well as your own. If you consult the individuals who are affected by your plans, you may find that they are surprisingly supportive, instead of being resentful of the extra time you are spending studying.

3 Next, give some thought to the times of day when you **work most effectively**. This differs very much from individual to individual. Some people can concentrate first thing in the morning. Others work best in the early evening, or last thing at night. Some people find their day-to-day work so demanding that they are unable to do anything extra during the week, but must concentrate their study time at weekends. Mark the times when you feel you could do your best work on the timetable. It is extremely important to acknowledge your personal preferences here. If you ignore them, you may devise a timetable that is completely unrealistic and which you will not be able to adhere to.

4 Consider your **other commitments**. Everybody has certain tasks, from doing the washing to walking the dog, that must be performed on a regular basis. These tasks may not have to be done at a particular time, but you should take them into consideration when planning your schedule. You may be able to find more convenient times to get these jobs done, or be able to persuade other people to help you with them.

5 Now mark some time for **relaxation**. If your timetable is to be sustainable, it must include some time for you to build up your reserves. If your normal week does not include any regular physical activity, make sure that you include some in your revision timetable. A couple of hours spent in a sports centre or swimming pool each week will probably enhance your ability to concentrate.

6 Your timetable should now be taking shape. You can probably see obvious study sessions emerging. It is not advisable to work for too long at any one session. Most people find that they can only really concentrate for one or two hours at a time. If your study sessions are longer than this, you should split them up.

What do I need to cover during my revision?

Most candidates are more confident about some parts of the syllabus than others. Before you begin your revision, it is important to have an overview of where your strengths and weaknesses lie.

One way to do this is to take a sheet of paper and divide it into three columns. Mark the columns:

OK **Marginal** **Not OK**

or use similar headings to indicate how confident you are with a topic. Then go through the syllabus (reprinted in Section 1) and list the topics under the appropriate headings. Alternatively, you could use the list of key topics in Section 5 of this book to compile your overview. You might also find it useful to skim through the introductions or summaries to the textbook or workbooks you have used in your course. These should remind you of parts of the course that you found particularly easy or difficult at the time. You could also use some of the exercises and questions in the workbooks or textbooks, or some of the questions in this book, as a diagnostic aid to discover the areas where you need to work hardest.

It is also important to be aware which areas of the syllabus are so central to the subject that they are likely to be examined in every diet, and which are more obscure, and not likely to come up so frequently. Your textbooks, workbooks and lecture notes will help you here. (You may also find it useful to read the guidance notes on the syllabus provided in Section 8.) Remember, the Examiner will be looking for broad coverage of the syllabus. There is no point in knowing one or two topics in exhaustive detail if you do so at the expense of the rest of the course.

Writing your revision timetable

3

You now have the information you need to write your timetable. You know how many weeks you have available, and the approximate amount of time that is available in each week.

You should stop all serious revision 48 hours before your examination. After this point, you may want to look back at your notes to refresh your memory, but you should not attempt to revise any new topics. A clear and rested brain is worth more than any extra facts you could memorise in this period.

Make one copy of this chart for each week you have available for revision.

Using your time planning chart, write in the times of your various study sessions during the week.

In the lower part of the chart, write in the topics that you will cover in each of these sessions.

Example of a revision timetable

Revision timetable Week beginning:							
	Monday	Tuesday	Wednesday	Thursday	Friday	Saturday	Sunday
Study sessions							
Topics							

Some revision techniques

There should be two elements in your revision. You must **look back** to the work you have covered in the course and **look forward** to the examination. The techniques you use should reflect these two aspects of revision.

3

Revision should not be boring. It is useful to try a variety of techniques. You probably already have some revision techniques of your own and you may also like to try some of the techniques suggested here, if they are new to you. However, don't waste time with methods of revision which are not effective for you.

- Go through your lecture notes, textbook or workbooks and use a highlighter pen to mark important points.
- Produce a new set of summarised notes. This can be a useful way of re-absorbing information, but you must be careful to keep your notes concise, or you may find that you are simply reproducing work you have done before. It is helpful to use a different format for your notes.
- Make a collection of key words which remind you of the essential concepts of a topic.
- Reduce your notes to a set of key facts and definitions which you must memorise. Write them on cards which you can keep with you all the time.
- When you come across areas which you were unsure about first time around, rework relevant questions in your course materials, then study the answers in great detail.
- If there are isolated topics which you feel are completely beyond you, identify exactly what it is that you cannot understand and find someone (such as a lecturer or recent graduate) who can explain these points to you.
- Practise as many exam standard questions as you can. The best way to do this is to work to time, under exam conditions. You should always resist looking at the answer until you have finished. As well as the questions in this book, you could use old ACCA examination papers. Many questions based on the old syllabus will provide useful practice.
- If you have come to rely on a word processor in your day-to-day work, you may have got out of the habit of writing at speed. It is worth reviving this skill before you sit down in the examination hall.
- If you have a plentiful supply of relevant questions, you could use them to practise planning answers, and then compare your notes with the answers provided. This is not a substitute for writing full answers, but can be helpful additional practice.
- Go back to questions you have already worked on during the course. This time, complete them under exam conditions, paying special attention to the layout and organisation of your answers. Then compare them in detail with the suggested answers and think about the ways in which your answer differs. This is a useful way of 'fine tuning' your technique.
- During your revision period, make a conscious effort to identify situations which illustrate concepts and ideas that may arise in the examination. These situations could come from your own work, or from reading the quality press. This technique will give you a new perspective on your studies and could also provide material which you can use in the examination.

EXAMINATION TECHNIQUES

The examination

This section is divided into two parts. The first part considers the practicalities of sitting the examination. If you have taken other ACCA examinations recently, you may find that everything here is familiar to you. The second part discusses some examination techniques which you may find useful.

The practicalities

What to take with you

You should make sure that you have:

- your ACCA registration card
- your ACCA registration docket.

You may also take to your desk:

- pens and pencils
- a ruler and slide rule
- a calculator
- charting template and geometrical instruments
- eraser and correction fluid.

You are not allowed to take rough paper into the examination.

If you take any last-minute notes with you to the examination hall, make sure these are not on your person. You should keep notes or books in your bag or briefcase, which you will be asked to leave at the side of the examination hall.

Although most examination halls will have have a clock, it is advisable to wear a watch, just in case your view is obscured.

If your calculator is solar-powered, make sure it works in artificial light. Some examination halls are not particularly well-lit. If you use a battery-powered calculator, take some spare batteries with you. For obvious reasons, you may not use a calculator which has a graphic/word display memory. Calculators with printout facilities are not allowed because they could disturb other candidates.

Getting there

You should arrange to arrive at the examination hall at least half an hour before the examination is due to start. If the hall is a large one, the invigilator will start filling the hall half an hour before the starting time.

Make absolutely sure that you know how to get to the examination hall and how long it will take you. Check on parking or public transport. Leave yourself enough time so that you will not be anxious if the journey takes a little longer than you anticipated. Many people like to make a practice trip the day before their first examination.

4

At the examination hall

Examination halls differ greatly in size. Some only hold about ten candidates. Others can sit many hundreds of people. You may find that more than one examination is being taken at the hall at the same time, so don't panic if you hear people discussing a completely different subject from the one you have revised.

While you are waiting to go in, don't be put off by other people talking about how well, or badly, they have prepared for the examination.

You will be told when to come in to the examination hall. The desks are numbered. (Your number will be on your examination docket.) You will be asked to leave any bags at the side of the hall.

Inside the hall, the atmosphere will be extremely formal. The invigilator has certain things which he or she must tell candidates, often using a particular form of words. Listen carefully, in case there are any unexpected changes to the arrangements.

On your desk you will see a question paper and an answer booklet in which to write your answers. You will be told when to turn over the paper.

During the examination

You will have to leave your examination paper and answer booklet in the hall at the end of the examination. It is quite acceptable to write on your examination paper if it helps you to think about the questions. However, all workings should be in your answers. You may write any plans and notes in your answer booklet, as long as you cross them out afterwards.

If you require a new answer booklet, put your hand up and a supervisor will come and bring you one.

At various times during the examination, you will be told how much time you have left.

You should not need to leave the examination hall until the examination is finished. Put up your hand if you need to go to the toilet, and a supervisor will accompany you. If you feel unwell, put up your hand, and someone will come to your assistance. If you simply get up and walk out of the hall, you will not be allowed to re-enter.

Before you finish, you must fill in the required information on the front of your answer booklet.

Examination techniques

Tackling Paper 11

You must answer four out of six questions. One of the aims of this paper is to consider the interrelationship of the various taxes. You should therefore expect most questions to deal with more than one tax.

The Examiner will be looking for broadly based knowledge of the taxation system, rather than minutely detailed knowledge of specific topics or taxes.

Some questions may ask you to restrict your answer to certain taxes. This will be done either to make it possible for you to answer the question in the time available or to avoid repetition within the paper. It is essential that you follow these instructions, as you will be given no marks for consideration of taxes which are specifically outside the scope of the question and will waste valuable time.

You will be given some tax rates and allowances on the paper. These are shown in Section 1 of this book. You should be aware of what information you will, and will not, be provided with.

Your general strategy

You should spend the first ten minutes of the examination reading the paper. If you have a choice of question, decide which questions you will do. You must divide the time you spend on questions in proportion to the marks on offer. Don't be tempted to spend more time on a question you know a lot about, or one which you find particularly difficult. If a question has more than one part, you must complete each part.

On every question, the first marks are the easiest to gain. Even if things go wrong with your timing and you don't have time to complete a question properly, you will probably gain some marks by making a start.

Spend the last five minutes reading through your answers and making any additions or corrections.

You may answer written questions in any order you like. Some people start with their best question, to help them relax. Another strategy is to begin with your second best question, so that you are working even more effectively when you reach the question you are most confident about.

Once you have embarked on a question, you should try to stay with it, and not let your mind stray to other questions on the paper. You can only concentrate on one thing at once. However, if you get completely stuck with a question, leave space in your answer book and return to it later.

Answering the question

All Examiners say that the most frequent reason for failure in examinations, apart from basic lack of knowledge, is candidates' unwillingness to answer the question that the Examiner has asked. A great many people include every scrap of knowledge they have on a topic, just in case it is relevant. Stick to the question and tailor your answer to what you are asked. Pay particular attention to the verbs in the question.

You should be particularly wary if you come across a question which appears to be almost identical to one which you have practised during your revision. It probably isn't! Wishful thinking makes many people see the question they would like to see on the paper, not the one that is actually there.

Read a question at least twice before you begin your answer. Underline key words on the question paper, if it helps focus your mind on what is required.

If you don't understand what a question is asking, state your assumptions. Even if you do not answer in precisely the way the Examiner hoped, you may be given some credit, if your assumptions are reasonable.

Presentation

You should do everything you can to make things easy for the marker. Although you will not be marked on your handwriting, the marker will find it easier to identify the points you have made if your answers are legible. The same applies to spelling and grammar. Use blue or black ink. The marker will be using red or green.

Use the margin to clearly identify which question, or part of a question you are answering.

Start each answer on a new page. The order in which you answer the questions does not matter, but if a question has several parts, these parts should appear in the correct order in your answer book.

If there is the slightest doubt when an answer continues on another page, indicate to the marker that he or she must turn over. It is irritating for a marker to think he or she has reached the end of an answer, only to turn the page and find that the answer continues.

Use columnar layouts for computations. This will help you to avoid mistakes, and is easier to follow.

Use headings and numbered sentences if they help to show the structure of your answer. However, don't write your answers in one-word note form.

It is a good idea to make a rough plan of an answer before you begin to write. Do this in your answer booklet, but make sure you cross it out neatly afterwards. The marker needs to be clear whether he or she is looking at your rough notes, or the answer itself.

Computations

Before you begin a computation, you may find it helpful to jot down the stages you will go through. Cross out these notes afterwards.

It is essential to include all your workings and to indicate where they fit in to your answer. It is important that the marker can see where you got the figures in your answer from. Even if you make mistakes in your computations, you will be given credit for using a principle correctly, if it is clear from your workings and the structure of your answer.

If you spot an arithmetical error which has implications for figures later in your answer, it may not be worth spending a lot of time reworking your computation.

If you are asked to comment or make recommendations on a computation, you must do so. There are important marks to be gained here. Even if your computation contains mistakes, you may still gain marks if your reasoning is correct.

Use the layouts which you see in the answers given in this booklet and in model answers. A clear layout will help you avoid errors and will impress the marker.

Essay questions

You must plan an essay before you start writing. One technique is to quickly jot down any ideas which you think are relevant. Re-read the question and cross out any points in your notes which are not relevant. Then number your points. Remember to cross out your plan afterwards.

Your essay should have a clear structure. It should contain a brief introduction, a main section and a conclusion. Don't waste time by restating the question at the start of your essay.

Break your essay up into paragraphs. Use sub-headings and numbered sentences if they help show the structure of your answer.

Be concise. It is better to write a little about a lot of different points than a great deal about one or two points.

The Examiner will be looking for evidence that you have understood the syllabus and can apply your knowledge in new situations. You will also be expected to give opinions and make judgements. These should be based on reasoned and logical arguments.

Reports, memos and other documents

Some questions ask you to present your answer in the form of a report or a memo or other document. It is important that you use the correct format – there are easy marks to be gained here. Adopt the format used in sample questions, or use the format you are familiar with in your day-to-day work, as long as it contains all the essential elements.

You should also consider the audience for any document you are writing. How much do they know about the subject? What kind of information and recommendations are required? The Examiner will be looking for evidence that you can present your ideas in an appropriate form.

SECTION

5

KEY REVISION TOPICS

The aim of this section is to provide you with a checklist of key information relating to this Paper. You should use it as a reminder of topics to be revised rather than as a summary of all you need to know. Aim to revise as many topics as possible because many of the questions in the exam draw on material from more than one section of the syllabus. You will get more out of this Section if you read through Section 3, *General Revision Guidance* first.

Paper 11 is very much concerned with identifying elections and reliefs that will minimise a taxpayer's liability. In this Section we will be looking briefly at some of the most important claims that can be made, revising any conditions that must be met, and identifying the relevant time limits. All sections refer to ICTA 1988, unless otherwise stated.

1 Schedule E

Income is charged on the receipts basis. Expenses are only deductible if incurred 'wholly, exclusively and necessarily in the performance of the duties'.

Directors and employees earning in excess of £8,500 p.a. are assessable on benefits in kind. The charge is based on the cost to the employer. Cost means marginal cost (*Pepper* v *Hart*).

Class 1 National Insurance, both employers and employees, is chargeable on payments of salary and all cash benefits. In addition, if employees are provided with company cars, the employer pays class 1A NIC based on the car and fuel benefit charges. The car benefit charge is now based on the list price of the car.

2 Schedule DI profits

The following types of expenditure are not deductible in computing schedule DI profits:

- capital items
- appropriations of profit
- annual charges
- entertaining
- expenditure not incurred wholly and exclusively for the purpose of the trade.

Pre-trading expenditure is allowable if revenue in nature and incurred within seven years of the commencement of trading. For companies it is treated as if incurred on the first day of trading. For individuals it is treated as a loss arising in the first year of assessment.

For businesses commencing before 6 April 1994 the schedule DI commencement rules are:

	Statutory	*Taxpayer's s62 election*
Year 1	Actual	–
Year 2	First 12 months	Actual
Year 3	PYB or First 12 months	Actual

The s62 election must be made within seven years of the end of the second year of assessment.

The schedule DI cessation rules are:

	Statutory	*Revenue's s63 election*
Final	Actual	–
Penultimate	PYB	Actual
Pre-penultimate	PYB	Actual

Businesses commencing on or after 6 April 1994 will be subject to the new current year basis of assessment. The assessment will be based on the profits for the accounting year ending in the year of assessment.

In the first year, the profits to be assessed will be those arising in the year to 5 April. The normal current year basis will apply from the second year of assessment onwards.

The profits assessable in the final year of assessment are those arising from the end of the basis period assessed in the penultimate year of assessment until the date of cessation.

The commencement rules still mean that it is possible for some profits to be taken into account in more than one year of assessment. Such profits will be eligible for overlap relief. This relief will be given either when the business ceases, or for any earlier year of assessment for which the basis period is longer than twelve months.

3 Capital allowances

On commencement, where basis periods overlap, expenditure will be allocated to the earliest possible period. On cessation, the gap must be allocated to the following basis period, unless this is the final year of assessment, in which case it must be allocated to the preceding basis period.

If a business is sold to a connected person, the transferor and transferee can jointly elect to transfer the assets at their written down values, rather than at their market values. This election must be made within two years of the date of the transfer.

A depooling election can be made in respect of short-life assets. The election must be made within two years of the end of the basis period in which the expenditure is incurred, and the asset must be disposed of within four years of the end of the basis period in which the expenditure is incurred. The election is beneficial if the asset is expected to be sold at a loss.

Under the new current year basis of assessment, capital allowances will be treated as trading expenses. They will thus be deductible in computing the schedule DI profit, in the same way as currently applies for corporation tax purposes.

Capital allowances will be calculated in respect of accounting periods rather than basis periods.

4 Trading losses (income tax)

These are the options available to a taxpayer who incurs a trading loss:

s385 – carry forward and set against future profits of the same trade. Claim within six years of the year of the loss.

s380 – set against statutory total income of the year of the loss and/or the following year. Claim within two years of the end of the fiscal year for which relief is claimed.

Capital allowances may increase a s380 claim, or may be carried forward separately under s385.

s72 FA 1991 – after a s380 claim has been made, any remaining loss can be set against capital gains for the same year. The loss is treated as a capital loss for that year. Claim within two years of the end of the fiscal year for which relief is claimed.

s381 – losses arising in the first four years of trading may be carried back on a last in first out basis, and set against statutory total income of the three preceding years. The loss must be computed using the statutory basis and the claim must be made within two years of the end of the fiscal year for which relief is claimed.

s388 – losses arising in the final twelve months of trading may be carried back and set against trading profits of the three preceding fiscal years. Claim within six years of the end of the fiscal year in which the trade ceased.

5 Partnerships

A brand new partnership is subject to the normal schedule DI commencement rules. When a new partnership arises as a result of a change in membership the special DI commencement rules apply. Under these, the first four years of trading are assessed on an actual basis, with the s62 election applying to years five and six. Partnerships commencing on or after 6 April 1994 will be assessed using the new current year basis of assessment. Under these new rules, a change in the membership of a partnership will no longer be regarded as a cessation for tax purposes.

A s113(2) continuation election can be made in the following circumstances:

- a sole trader takes someone into partnership
- a change in the membership of a partnership occurs
- a partnership reverts to being a sole trader.

The election must be signed by all the partners, both before and after the change, within two years of the date of the change.

When a change in the membership of a partnership occurs on or after 6 April 1994, making a s113(2) election will avoid the immediate application of the new current year basis of assessment.

Where a partnership suffers a loss, it will be allocated between the partners according to the type of loss relief claimed:

- under s380 the loss is allocated according to the profit sharing ratio in force during the fiscal year in which the loss is made

- under s385 the loss is allocated according to the profit sharing ratio of the accounting period in which the loss arose.

6 CGT – holdover and rollover reliefs

A taxpayer can claim holdover relief in respect of gifts of the following assets:

- business assets used for the purpose of the trade
- shares in an unquoted or personal trading company
- property resulting in an immediate charge to inheritance tax.

A claim for holdover relief must normally be made jointly by the donor and donee.

Rollover relief is available in respect of disposals and replacements of the following assets:

5

- ▶ land and buildings occupied for the purpose of the trade
- ▶ fixed plant and machinery
- ▶ goodwill.

The replacement asset must be purchased within the period beginning one year before and ending three years after the disposal. The claim must be made within six years of the end of the year of assessment in which the disposal occurs.

An individual can claim reinvestment relief in respect of any chargeable gains. To qualify for relief, the gains must be reinvested in an unquoted trading company in the period beginning one year before and ending three years after the disposal. There is no requirement for the investor to take a minimum holding in the company.

Unlike other forms of holdover/rollover reliefs, it is not necessary to re-invest the full sale proceeds in order to obtain full relief. Instead, it is only necessary to reinvest the full amount of the gain. It is also possible to specify the amount of gain to be rolled over. This allows the taxpayer to make use of the annual exemption and any capital losses.

7 CGT – reliefs available on the disposal of a business

Retirement relief is available to an individual aged 55 or over, who disposes of all or part of a business, or shares in a personal trading company. A personal trading company is one in which the individual owns at least 5% of the share capital and is a full-time working director or employee.

Relief is only available in respect of gains on chargeable business assets. The first £250,000 of the gain is tax free; 50% of the gain between £250,000 and £1,000,000 is tax free. These limits are apportioned if the individual has satisfied the ownership and employment conditions for less than ten years. Retirement relief is given before reinvestment relief.

If a sole trader transfers his business to a limited company, a form of hold over relief is given automatically, provided:

- ▶ the business is transferred as a going concern
- ▶ all of the business assets (with the possible exception of cash) are transferred
- ▶ the consideration for the transfer is wholly or mainly in shares.

The capital gain is computed as normal and then the amount held over is computed by applying the formula: Capital gain × Value of shares/Total consideration. The balance of the gain remains chargeable. If a chargeable gain is required, this can be generated by taking part of the consideration in the form of cash, or leaving it outstanding on loan account. The optimum amount of cash consideration can be computed using the formula: Total consideration × Chargeable gain required/Total capital gain.

8 IHT – exemptions

The following transfers are wholly exempt, whether made during lifetime or on death:

5

- transfers between spouses (limited to a cumulative total of £55,000 if the spouse is non-UK domiciled)
- gifts to UK charities
- gifts to qualifying political parties.

The following lifetime transfers are wholly or partly exempt:

- small gifts of up to £250 per donee per year
- normal expenditure out of income
- gifts in consideration of marriage (£5,000 by a parent, £2,500 by one party to the other, £2,500 by a grandparent or remoter ancestor, £1,000 by anyone else).

The annual exemption of £3,000 per year may be carried forward for one year if unused.

A potentially exempt transfer (PET) is any lifetime transfer of value made by an individual to:

- another individual
- an accumulation and maintenance trust
- a trust for the disabled
- a trust with an interest in possession.

PETs are exempt unless the transferor dies within seven years. All other transfers (eg transfers into discretionary trusts) are chargeable lifetime transfers (CLT). They are charged at half the death rate, at the time of the transfer.

9 IHT – business and agricultural property relief

Business property relief (BPR) may be claimed in respect of the following lifetime or death transfers:

- the whole or part of a business or an interest in a business (100%)
- a holding of more than 25% (including related property) in unquoted or USM shares (100%)
- a holding of less than 25% in quoted or USM shares (50%)
- quoted shares in, or securities of, a company controlled by the transferor (50%)
- assets used for business purposes (50%).

Relief is not due if a binding contract for sale has been entered into by the transferor at the time of the transfer.

To qualify for BPR the property must have been owned by the transferor throughout the two years prior to the transfer. If the transfer was a PET which becomes chargeable, relief is only given if the transferee still owns the property at the date of the transferor's death.

Agricultural property relief (APR) is given in respect of:

- property with vacant possession occupied by the transferor throughout the two years prior to the transfer (100%)
- tenanted property owned for seven years prior to the transfer (50%).

10 IHT – calculating the tax due

5

The value placed on property for IHT purposes is the loss to the donor's estate. Related property (belonging to a spouse) is taken into account if its inclusion would give a higher value than otherwise obtained.

Unit trusts are valued at the lower of the two prices quoted. Shares are valued at the lower of:

- their quarter up price
- the average of the highest and lowest marked bargains.

The amount of tax due on a CLT depends on whether the donor or the donee is going to pay the tax. If the donee is going to pay, the tax due is: CLT × 20%. If the donor is going to pay, the tax due is: CLT × 20/80.

The normal due date for payment of IHT on a CLT is:

- 30 April of the year following the transfer, if made between 6 April and 30 September
- six months after the end of the month of transfer, in all other cases.

On death, the tax is due six months after the end of the month of death. The donee must pay any IHT due as a result of a PET becoming chargeable. Taper relief is available to reduce the IHT due on transfers made more than three years before the date of death:

Years between gift and death	*Reduction in IHT*
3 – 4	20%
4 – 5	40%
5 – 6	60%
6 – 7	80%

11 IHT – adjustments after death and varying a will

If quoted investments are sold at a loss within 12 months of the date of death, a claim may be made to reduce the estate value by the amount of the loss. All investments disposed of within this period must be taken into account. The gross sale proceeds are used in the calculation.

If land is sold at a loss within four years of the date of death, a claim may be made to reduce the estate value by the amount of the loss. All land sold within this period must be taken into account provided that it is sold to an unconnected person, and the difference between the estate value and the gross sale proceeds exceeds the lower of £1,000 and 5% of the estate value.

In both these cases, if the sale proceeds are reinvested, the loss is restricted by the formula:

Loss × Amount reinvested/Gross sale proceeds.

A will may be varied after death by a deed of family arrangement. This must be made by the persons who were due to benefit under the will. It must be done in writing, without consideration, within two years of the date of death. It must be submitted to the Inspector within six months of the date of the deed. The variation is treated as if made by the deceased.

5

12 Trusts

Income tax – discretionary trusts pay income tax at the rate of 35%. All other trusts pay income tax at the basic rate of 25% (apart from on dividend income which is taxed at the lower rate of 20%). Trust expenses and personal allowances are not deductible in computing the trust's basic rate liability.

CGT – each trust has an annual exemption of £2,900 to set against any chargeable gains.

IHT – transfers to discretionary trusts are CLTs. Property in these trusts is subject to an IHT charge of a maximum of 6% at ten-yearly intervals. There is also an exit charge when property leaves the trust.

Distributions to beneficiaries – beneficiaries of trusts with an interest in possession receive income net of 25% tax. Beneficiaries of discretionary trusts receive income net of 35% tax.

13 Value added tax

A person is required to register for VAT within 30 days if:

- at the end of any month, the value of his taxable supplies over the previous twelve months exceeded £45,000, or
- at any time there are grounds for believing that the value of taxable supplies within the next 30 days will exceed £45,000.

A person must deregister within 30 days of the cessation of trading. There is a deemed self-supply, which can be avoided if the business is transferred as a going concern.

Input tax is not deductible in respect of:

- motor cars
- entertaining
- goods purchased and resold before the date of registration
- services received more than six months before the date of registration.

Two special schemes exist to reduce the burden of VAT on the small business:

- The annual accounting scheme available to businesses with a taxable turnover below £300,000 p.a. requires payment of 90% of the estimated liability throughout the year. The balance is submitted with the annual return within two months of the end of the accounting period; thus reducing administration costs.
- The cash accounting scheme for businesses with a taxable turnover below £350,000 p.a. allows the business to account for VAT on the basis of cash paid and received. Thus providing a cash flow advantage and automatic relief for bad debts.

14 Corporation tax losses

There are a number of options open to a company which makes a trading loss:

s393(1) – carry forward the loss and set it against future profits of the same trade. Claim within six years of the end of the loss making accounting period.

s393A – set the loss against profits of the same accounting period, before the deduction of any charges. Then carry back any balance three years on a last in first out basis, setting it against profits after the deduction of trading charges. Claim within two years of the end of the accounting period in which the loss was incurred.

s242 – after a s393A claim has been made, any remaining loss can be set against surplus franked investment income of the same years as the s393A claim. Claim within the same time limits.

There are anti-avoidance provisions in s768 restricting the carry forward of losses after a change in ownership:

- If, within three years of the change in ownership, there is a major change in the nature or conduct of the trade, losses incurred before the change in ownership cannot be carried forward against profits arising after the change in ownership. These provisions also prevent the carry back of losses to accounting periods prior to a change in ownership.
- The carry forward of losses is also prevented if a company's trade has become small or negligible and a change in ownership occurs before there is a significant revival.

15 Surplus ACT

The maximum offset of ACT is computed by multipying the chargeable profits by the rate of ACT (currently 20%). ACT paid in excess of this figure is surplus ACT. There are three ways of dealing with surplus ACT:

- Carry it back six years on a last in first out basis, subject to the maximum offset in each year. Claim within two years of the end of the accounting period in which the surplus arose.
- Surrender the ACT to a company which was a 51% subsidiary throughout the accounting period in which the ACT was paid. Claim within six years of the end of the accounting period to which the surrender claim relates.
- Carry forward indefinitely.

From 1 July 1994, companies can elect to pay a Foreign Income Dividend (FID) out of foreign source profits. Surplus ACT arising from the payment of a FID will be recoverable. The shareholder receiving the FID will be treated as receiving income net of 20% tax. However, non-taxpayers will not be able to reclaim any tax as the FID does not carry a tax credit as such.

Companies falling within the definition of an International Headquarters Company (IHC) will not be required to pay ACT on FIDs at all. An IHC is a company with none of its shareholders owning less than 5% of its share capital and at least 80% of its shares being held by non-UK residents.

Anti-avoidance provisions exist to prevent the set off of ACT after a change of ownership in the same circumstances as those mentioned above in respect of trading losses.

16 Associated companies and 51% groups

Companies are associated if, at any time within an accounting period, one is under the control of the other or both are under common control. A company does not have to be UK resident to be associated. Associated companies share

5

the upper and lower limits for small companies' rate taxation equally between them.

A 51% group exists where one company owns more than 50% of the ordinary share capital of another, or both are more than 50% owned by the same UK resident company. Subsubsidiaries may be included within the group provided that the parent company has an effective interest of more than 50%.

Members of a 51% group can:

- ▶ Elect to pay dividends between group members without accounting for ACT (group income election).
- ▶ Elect to pay charges between group members without accounting for income tax (the charges are then paid gross).
- ▶ Surrender ACT from a holding company down to a subsidiary.

17 75% groups

A 75% group exists for capital gains tax purposes if a parent holds more than 75% of the ordinary share capital of a subsidiary. Subsubsidiaries are also included provided that the parent's effective interest is more than 50%. All companies must be UK resident and none can be a member of more than one group.

Members of a 75% CGT group can:

- ▶ Transfer chargeable assets between each other on a no gain, no loss basis. A chargeable gain will only arise when the asset finally leaves the group or when a company leaves the group within six years of receiving an asset by way of a no gain, no loss transfer.
- ▶ Be treated as a single trade for the purpose of making rollover relief claims.

A 75% group exists for the purpose of transferring trading losses if a parent has an effective interest of more than 75% in a subsidiary or subsubsidiary. All companies must be UK resident. It is possible for a company to be a member of more than one of this type of 75% group.

Members of this type of 75% group may transfer trading losses between group members. The losses may only be transferred in respect of a corresponding accounting period. The maximum that may be surrendered to any one company is the lower of the amount of the loss and the amount of the claimant company's chargeable profits. A claim must be made within two years of the end of the surrendering company's accounting period. The claim is made by the claimant company, with the consent of the surrendering company.

18 Consortia

A company is a consortium owned company if at least 75% of its ordinary share capital is owned by UK resident companies, each owning at least 5% and not more than 75%.

Members of a consortium may:

- ▶ Make a group income election.
- ▶ Transfer trading losses between the COC and members of the consortium. The maximum claim is an amount equivalent to the percentage of ordinary share capital held by that consortium member.

Claims to transfer losses must be made within two years of the end of the surrendering company's loss making accounting period.

19 Overseas aspects of personal taxation

Income tax – UK residents are liable to UK income tax on their worldwide income. However, a UK resident individual who is non-UK domiciled can only be taxed on overseas income to the extent that it is remitted to the UK. Non-UK residents are only liable to UK income tax on their UK income.

CGT – UK residents are liable to UK CGT on their worldwide assets. Non-UK residents are not liable to UK CGT, unless they carry on a trade or profession in the UK, in which case they are liable to UK CGT on disposals of business assets situated in the UK.

IHT – liability to UK IHT is dependent on domicile not residence. UK domiciled individuals are liable to UK IHT on their worldwide assets. Non-UK domiciled individuals are only liable to UK IHT on assets situated in the UK. The definition of domicile for IHT purposes is extended to include:

- persons resident in the UK for 17 out of the preceding 20 fiscal years, ending with the year of the transfer, and
- persons who were UK domiciled at any time within the three years immediately preceding the year of the transfer.

20 Overseas aspects of corporate taxation

All companies incorporated in the UK are resident in the UK for corporation tax purposes. Companies not incorporated in the UK are treated as UK resident if their central management and control is in the UK. Companies which are resident in the UK, but which would be regarded as resident in another country for the purposes of a double taxation agreement, are treated as not resident in the UK.

UK resident companies are liable to UK corporation tax on their worldwide profits. A non-UK resident company is liable to UK corporation tax only on chargeable profits of a UK branch or agency.

A *controlled foreign company* (CFC) is a company resident outside the UK, controlled by persons resident within the UK and subject to a lower level of taxation in the country in which it is resident. A lower level of taxation is less than 3/4 of the corresponding UK tax.

The profits of a CFC are apportioned to UK corporate shareholders unless the CFC distributes at least 50% of its available profits within 18 months of the end of its accounting period.

21 Double taxation relief

When foreign income is received net of foreign tax, it must be grossed up in computing the income liable to UK tax. Once the UK tax liability has been computed, credit for the overseas tax suffered is then given. This credit is the lower of:

- the foreign tax suffered, and
- the UK tax due on that source of income.

5

For corporation tax purposes, double tax relief is deducted prior to setting off ACT. The maximum set off of ACT must be computed in respect of each source of income and is limited to the lower of:

- the taxable profits multiplied by the ACT percentage
- the CT liability remaining after the deduction of DTR.

22 Personal finance

Before advising on the suitability of an investment, an adviser must consider the client's marginal rate of tax, attitude to risk, need for liquidity, available funds, etc.

The following investments all attract some form of tax incentive:

Personal Pension Scheme – contributions are limited to a percentage of the individual's net relevant earnings. The percentage is determined by the individual's age at the beginning of that fiscal year. Contributions are deductible in computing statutory total income. The pension cannot be drawn until after the age of 50.

Life assurance – a qualifying policy must be for a term of at least ten years. The benefits paid out on maturity are free of both income tax and CGT. There is no maximum investment and no tax relief for the premiums paid.

Enterprise Investment Scheme – income tax relief at 20% is given in respect of new equity investment up to £100,000 in qualifying unquoted trading companies. Relief is not available to investors connected with the company (owning more than 30% of the issued share capital). However, an investor can become a paid director once the shares have been issued, and still qualify for relief. On the first disposal of shares acquired under the scheme, any gain will be exempt from CGT. Any loss may be claimed against either income or capital gains.

Personal equity plans – these allow the investment of a maximum £6,000 per fiscal year and/or £3,000 into a single company PEP. The plan manager invests in UK or EC equities. There is no relief for the initial investment, but income and gains on investments held within the PEP are free of both income tax and CGT. There is no minimum period of investment.

TESSAs – the account must remain open for five years and capital cannot be withdrawn during this period. Interest can be withdrawn less an amount equivalent to the basic rate of income tax. The maximum investment is £3,000 in the first year; over the five years the total maximum is £9,000. Interest is free of income tax provided that the rules are not breached.

Dividends – these now attract a tax credit of 20%. Basic rate taxpayers have no further liability. Higher rate taxpayers have to account for the difference between the higher and lower rates. Dividends are treated as the top slice of income.

Gilts – these are exempt from CGT on disposal.

ANALYSIS OF PAST PAPERS

Although June 1994 is the first examination based on the new ACCA syllabus, certain topics are similar to those in the old syllabus. In such a case, an analysis of past papers is very helpful in providing an idea of the type of question asked. However, you should be careful not to 'question spot' i.e. try to guess which topics will be included in the examination. Only a thorough understanding of all topics in the syllabus will ensure your success.

When looking at old syllabus exam papers, bear in mind that there has been a slight change of emphasis to tax planning; there is also slightly less emphasis on VAT and NI in Paper 11 – these have now moved to Paper 7.

As far as content is concerned, the main difference between the new Tax Planning paper and the old Advanced Taxation paper is the introduction of personal finance to the syllabus. A good example of the type of question you can expect on this topic is provided by Question 1 of the Pilot Paper.

When reviewing past Advanced Taxation papers, you should be aware that the style of questions has altered slightly. Questions under the old syllabus tended to require the discussion and computation of a taxpayer's liability based on the information given. Questions under the new syllabus will still require this but will, in addition, require you to identify suitable opportunities for minimising or deferring the liability.

SECTION

7

STUDENTS' NEWSLETTER ARTICLES

The *Students' Newsletter* regularly carries articles on accountancy, law and taxation and it is in your own interests to read these thoroughly as the contents may be relevant to a question in the examination.

CORPORATION TAX LOSS RELIEF

CAPITAL LOSSES, TRADING LOSSES AND GROUP RELIEF

By Anita Monteith

It is likely that any Paper 7 or Paper 11 exam will have at least one question on corporation tax. For the purposes of your exam, these questions tend to be centred around one major area, and popular problems include:

- *a long period of account*
- *the payment of tax, perhaps under the quarterly accounting system*
- *losses.*

Obviously there are likely to be other areas involved, but if you revise each of these carefully, you should gain some easy marks on the corporation tax questions. This article deals with the last of these problems, together with some other favourite topics which examiners like to combine with such questions.

Companies may suffer several different types of loss, and the relief available depends on the source.

Capital losses

Capital losses are calculated in the same way as capital gains. A company will first set off its capital losses against gains made in the same accounting period, and then carry forward any surplus net losses. Remember that companies pay corporation tax on their chargeable gains, and not capital gains tax.

Companies may not group relieve their capital losses.

Losses from letting property

Losses from letting unfurnished property in the UK can be relieved by companies in the same way as by individuals. The diagram in Appendix 1 summarises the possibilities.

Losses from letting furnished property are carried forward and relieved against future Schedule D Case VI income. Exceptionally, where a company is letting furnished holiday accommodation, the losses may be relieved as trading losses.

Trading losses

A company which has been trading on a commercial basis, with a view to realising a profit, may instead find itself in the position of having made a loss. The amount of the loss is calculated in exactly the same way as a profit would have been, and would include capital allowances.

For Paper 7, there are three reliefs of which you should be aware, to which you should add group relief for Paper 11. We will now consider each of these in turn.

Section 393(1) ICTA 1988

This allows for an unrelieved trading loss to be carried forward and set off automatically against trading profits of future years. The loss will be relieved as soon as possible, and it may be that charges paid in that future year are displaced, and themselves become unrelieved, as a result.

Section 393(9) ICTA 1988

Unrelieved trade charges can be carried forward and then relieved in much the same way as trading losses described above. This would cover such items as debenture interest paid by the company, patent and copyright royalties.

For the purposes of your exams, there is little to be gained by keeping the losses and charges being carried forward by the company separate. You need only keep a memorandum of the total amounts involved.

Section 393(A) ICTA 1988

Relief under this section is against a company's total profits of the accounting period in which the loss was suffered, and then against those of the preceding 36 months. There are, however, more detailed conditions of which you should be aware.

When claiming Section 393(A) relief in the current period, the loss is set against the company's total income and gains, before deducting any charges. The relief is then all or nothing; the company may not restrict the amount of loss relieved, for example in order to keep enough income in charge to tax for the set off of non-business charges.

The extension of the claim against the profits of the preceding 36 months is against the company's total income and gains, which are, for this purpose, after deducting business charges. Rather than just learning this rule by rote, think of it as making sense! After all there is little point taking back a trading loss, only to cause unrelieved business charges in an earlier year, which in turn would be brought forward for relief. You would find yourself working in circles!

The carry-back claim described above can only be made if the current claim has already been made. The company therefore has the following range of options:

Profits of	*Options* 1	2	3
Current period	Claim (1)	Claim	No claim
Preceding 36 months	Claim (2)	No claim	No claim

When carrying back the loss for relief, it will always be set against the profits of the latest period first.

These rules are illustrated by the example in Appendix 2.

Note that, had the company changed its accounting date during the preceding 36 months, it would have been necessary to apportion its profits available in the earliest period.

Exam technique is very important when answering losses questions. The computations are easier to deal with in columns, and you must be careful not to add in unrelieved charges to be carried forward until you have finished carrying the trading losses back.

Group relief

This relief is only examined in the Paper 11 syllabus, and the key rules can be summarised as follows:

- Two or more companies are members of the same group, if one is a 75 per cent subsidiary of the other, or both are 75 per cent subsidiaries of a third.
- The relief is available from holding company to subsidiary, or vice versa, or between subsidiaries.
- Trading losses and any unrelieved charges can be surrendered, but not capital losses.
- Any amount of the surrendering company's loss, etc., can be group relieved, although the claimant company must be able to use the loss in that same period. If the companies have non-coterminous accounting periods, you will need a further working (see Appendix 3).
- The profits against which a group relieved loss can be set off are after deducting the claimant company's own charges, and its own losses either brought forward or of the current period.

When deciding on the best possible use for a group's losses, consider relieving any profits being taxed in the margin between the upper and lower limits first, and only then those being taxed at the large companies rate. Other aspects worthy of mention are cash flow, and certainty of relief by claiming relief for the loss immediately, rather than by carrying it forward.

Exam questions will usually contain rather more calculations than shown in the appendices to this article. You will be required to do extra workings, for example the capital allowances, to arrive at the profits and losses in the first instance. Nevertheless, the principles remain the same, and with practice should earn you some easy marks.

Appendix 1 – Use of Schedule A losses

Properties A, B, C, D and E are let on leases described as follows:

Property	
A and B	Full rent, landlord responsible for repairs
C and D	Full rent, tenant responsible for repairs
E	Nominal rent

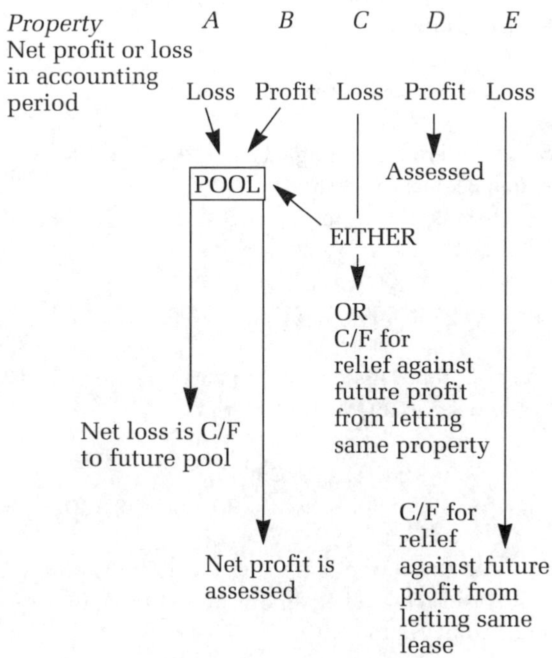

Appendix 2

The results of Loser plc for the past few years have been as follows:

	Year ended 31 March				
	1991	*1992*	*1993*	*1994*	*1995*
	£	£	£	£	£
Trading profit/(loss)	23,000	57,000	49,000	(165,000)	72,000
Schedule D Case III	9,900	12,500	30,000	7,200	4,800
Charges paid (gross)					
Debenture interest	(10,000)	(10,000)	(10,000)	(10,000)	(10,000)
Charitable covenant	(1,000)	(1,000)	(1,000)	(1,000)	(1,000)

The loss will be relieved as follows:

	Year ended 31 March				
	1991	*1992*	*1993*	*1994*	*1995*
	£	£	£	£	£
Schedule D Case I	23,000	57,000	49,000	Nil	72,000
Loss B/F S 393(1)					(16,400)
					55,600
Schedule D Case III	9,900	12,500	30,000	7,200	4,800
	32,900	69,500	79,000	7,200	60,400
S.393(A) - current				(7,200)	
Trade charges	(10,000)	(10,000)	(10,000)	–	(10,000)
S.393(A) carry back	(22,900)	(59,500)	(69,000)		
Non-trade charges	–	–	–	–	(1,000)
Profits chargeable to corporation tax	–	–	–	–	49,400

Loss memorandum		£
Loss suffered in year ended 31 March 1994		165,000
S.393A current relief		(7,200)
Carryback relief	1993	(69,000)
	1992	(59,500)
	1991	(22,900)
		6,400
Add unrelieved trade charges in 1994		10,000
		16,400
Relieved under S.393(1) ICTA 1988		(16,400)

Appendix 3

H Ltd prepares its accounts for calendar years. S Ltd prepares its accounts for years ended 31 March.

H Ltd had profits chargeable to corporation tax as follows:

	£
Year ended 31 December 1993	28,000
Year ended 31 December 1994	42,000

S Ltd suffered a trading loss of £36,600 in its year ended 31 March 1994.

The maximum loss that S Ltd can surrender for H Ltd to use in 1993 is the lower of:

28,000 × 9/12= 21,000

and (36,600) × 9/12= (27,450) i.e. 21,000

The maximum loss that S Ltd can surrender for H Ltd to use in 1994 is the lower of:

42,000 × 3/12= 10,500

and (36,600) × 3/12= (9,150) i.e. 9,150

Any amount of the loss up to these limits can be group relieved. The remaining £6,450 must be retained by S Ltd.

How the November 1993 Budget affects Paper 11 Tax Planning

By David Harrowven, Examiner

The aim of this article is to summarise the changes proposed in the November 1993 budget as they specifically affect Paper 11. For ease of reference, the changes have been summarised under the relevant headings of the syllabus.

Personal business taxation

The current year basis

For the self-employed presently assessed under Schedule D on the preceding year basis of taxation, there is to be a change to the current year basis as from 1997–98, with 1996–97 being the year of transition. This change will not be examinable at the December 1994 diet, although students should be aware that the change is imminent when, for example, providing taxation advice on whether or not to incorporate a business.

Although the new basis will apply immediately to new businesses commencing after 5 April 1994, a detailed computational question on this area *will not* be set at the December 1994 diet. The rules concerning businesses commencing to trade prior to 6 April 1994 are still examinable.

Capital gains tax

Retirement relief

The limits have been raised as from 30 November 1993 so that the first £250,000 of gains now qualify for relief, with 50% of gains between £250,000 and £1,000,000 also being exempt.

Reinvestment relief

Relief from CGT for entrepreneurs selling their own company and reinvesting in an unquoted trading company was introduced by the Finance Act 1993. This relief is extended from 30 November 1993 to any chargeable gains made by individuals. The relief is broadly similar to the existing relief as follows:

a) To qualify, the proceeds from the disposal must be reinvested in eligible shares in unquoted trading companies.
b) The reinvestment must take place within a period beginning one year before and ending three years after the date of disposal.
c) The main exclusions from relief are re-investments in companies which hold more than half of their total assets as land, and companies carrying on certain financial activities, farming, and property development.

d) There is no requirement for the taxpayer to take a minimum holding in the unquoted company. This differs from the existing relief where a 5% holding is required.
e) Relief given is withdrawn if within three years of acquiring the shares the taxpayer emigrates, or the company ceases to qualify.

Inheritance tax

Rates of tax
The rates of IHT and the nil rate threshold of £150,000 are unchanged.

Trusts

Reinvestment relief
The extension of reinvestment relief covered above also applies to disposal proceeds re-invested by trustees, unless the beneficiaries of the trust are not individuals.

Corporate taxation

The audit requirement
The audit requirement for companies with a turnover of below £90,000 has been abolished, and companies with a turnover of between £90,000 and £350,000 will only require an independent accountant's report to verify that the accounts correctly reflect their books. This is an important consideration when deciding upon incorporation of a business.

Overseas activities

Foreign income dividend scheme (FIDS)
From 1 July 1994 companies can opt to pay a FID out of foreign source profits. The FID, which must be matched to profits of the same year, the previous year or subsequent years, will not carry a tax credit.

The aim of the FIDS is to help companies with surplus ACT problems. ACT will still be payable on the FID, but any surplus ACT resulting from the payment of the FID will now be recoverable.

The shareholder receiving the FID will be treated as receiving income net of 20% tax, and, as for normal dividends, there will be no further liability for 20% and 25% taxpayers. However, non-taxpayers will not be able to reclaim any tax as the FID does not carry a tax credit as such.

To increase the attractiveness of the UK as a base for companies, i.e. the European base of a multinational company, an International Headquarters Company (IHC) will not have to pay ACT on dividends at all. The definition of an IHC is a company with none of its shareholders owning less than 5% of its share capital, and at least 80% of its shares being held outside the United Kingdom.

Controlled foreign companies
The distribution test for non-trading controlled foreign companies has been altered from 90% of accounting profits to 90% of taxable profits. There is no change to the 50% test for trading companies.

Company residence
Companies which are resident in the UK, but which would be regarded as resident in another country for the purposes of a double taxation agreement, will in future be treated as not resident in the UK.

Personal finance

National Savings Pensioners Guaranteed Income Bond
A five-year fixed rate investment for pensioners is to be introduced. The interest paid by the bond will be taxable, although it will be paid gross, making it attractive to non-taxpayers.

The Enterprise Investment Scheme (EIS)
The EIS will replace the Business Expansion Scheme (which is no longer examinable), and will have the aim of providing equity financing to unquoted trading companies.

It will apply to new equity shares issued after 1 January 1994, and will allow a taxpayer to obtain tax relief at the rate of 20% on qualifying investments up to £100,000 per tax year. The scheme, which is broadly similar to the old BES, is as follows:

a) The first disposal of shares on which relief has not been withdrawn will be exempt from CGT.
b) Shares must be held for at least five years.
c) If a loss is made on the disposal of shares on which relief has not been withdrawn, relief will be available for the purposes of either income tax or CGT.
d) There is a limit of £1,000,000 on the amount that a company can raise in a year on which relief will be given.
e) Relief on half the amount an individual invests between 6 April and 5 October in any year can be carried back to the previous tax year, subject to a maximum of £15,000.
f) A qualifying investor is an individual who is not connected with the company (employees and shareholders with over 30% of the shares) during a specified period.
g) However, an investor can become a paid director and still qualify for relief if he or she was not connected with the company or its trade at any time before the eligible shares were issued.
h) The scheme applies to companies trading in the UK whether or not they are incorporated in the UK, and to investors who are liable to UK income tax whether or not they are resident in the UK.

i) The scheme will *not* apply to investment in private rented housing.

Venture capital trusts
Proposals for a new type of investment trust to invest in unquoted trading companies will not be examined at the December 1994 exam diet.

How the Finance Act 1994 affects Paper 11, Tax Planning

By David Harrowven, Examiner

The previous article covers the effect of the November 1993 budget on Paper 11, and was also published in the February 1994 Students' Newsletter. *The aim of this second article is to look at the more important changes in greater detail, consider some tax planning points, and highlight any amendments to the new legislation that have been made since the previous article. You should also refer to the preceding article in respect of the Finance Act 1994 changes as they affect Paper 7, The Tax Framework, since these changes will also have an impact on Paper 11.*

For ease of reference, the changes have been dealt with under the relevant headings of the syllabus.

Personal business taxation

The current year basis
As mentioned in the previous article, the new current year basis of assessment will apply immediately to new businesses commencing after 5 April 1994, although a *detailed computational question on this area will not be set* at the December 1994 diet. The basic rules of the new current year basis have been covered in the preceding article, so this article will concentrate on the more detailed aspects and consider some tax planning points.

Choice of accounting date
Under the old preceding year basis it was normally beneficial to choose an accounting date of just after, rather than just before, 5 April. This ensured the maximum interval between earning profits and having to pay the related tax liability. The same logic holds true for the new current year basis, although the interval will be 12 months shorter in each case. For example, accounts for the year ended 31 March 1996 will be assessed in 1995–96, with payment of tax due on 1 January 1996 and 1 July 1996, while accounts for the year ended 30 April 1996 would not be assessed until 1996–97, with payment of tax due on 1 January 1997 and 1 July 1997.

However, the down side of this choice of accounting date is that overlap profits are increased. Assuming that in each instance the business commenced trading on 1 April 1995, the opening years' assessments and overlap profits would be as follows:

Year ended 31 March 1996

1994–95	1 April 1995 to 5 April 1995
1995–96	1 April 1995 to 31 March 1996

Overlap profits are therefore effectively nil, being based on the five days that fall into 1994–95.

Period ended 30 April 1996

1994–95	1 April 1995 to 5 April 1995
1995–96	6 April 1995 to 5 April 1996
1996–97	1 May 1995 to 30 April 1996

Overlap profits are therefore for the 11-month period 1 May 1995 to 5 April 1996.

Although there is relief for overlap profits, there may be a long delay before relief is obtained if this is on the cessation of the business. The choice of accounting date is therefore not as clear-cut as previously.

Another tax planning point under the old preceding year basis was that it was usually beneficial to ensure that profits for the first period of trading were kept to a minimum, because they normally formed the basis period for more than one year of assessment. Profits could be minimised by, for example, renting equipment for the first period of trading rather than purchasing it, or by the payment of bonuses to employees. The same type of planning will also be applicable to the current year basis if there are overlap profits which will not be relieved for a number of years.

Capital allowances and losses
Capital allowances under the current year basis are to be treated as a business expense, rather than as a deduction against profits as under the preceding year basis. This is the basis already used for corporation tax purposes, and will be particularly relevant when considering relief for trading losses. Under the preceding year basis, capital allowances can be used at the taxpayer's option (s383 ICTA 1988) to augment or create a trading loss for relief against total income. Under the current year basis, the only way of restricting the amount of capital allowances to be included in a loss claim will be by disclaiming them, as in the following example:

Joe, who is single, has made a trading loss, before capital allowances, of £4,000 for the year ended 30 June 1996. On 1 March 1996 he bought new equipment costing £8,000. His profits for the year ended 30 June 1995 were £7,700 (assume that no capital allowances were available for this year). Joe has no other income or outgoings. Under the current year basis, losses can be claimed against total income of either the year of the loss (1996–97) or the *preceding* year (1995–96). His tax position, claiming maximum capital allowances of £2,000 (8,000 × 25%), would be:

	1995–96	*1996–97*
	£	*£*
Schedule D profits	7,700	–
Loss relief (4,000 + 2,000)	(6,000)	–
	1,700	–
Personal allowance	3,445	3,445
Taxable income	–	–

To avoid wasting Joe's personal allowance for 1995–96 it is necessary to disclaim capital allowances of £1,745 so that the loss relief claim becomes £4,255 (4,000 + (2,000 – 1,745)). The written down value carried forward is correspondingly increased by £1,745.

Under the rules applicable to the preceding year basis, it is possible to achieve exactly the same result, but alternatively it would be possible to simply claim the trading loss of £4,000 against total income, leave a small profit of £255 (7,700 – 4,000 – 3,445), and carry forward the capital allowances of £2,000 as a loss to be set off against future trading profits. This loss carried forward will often be more beneficial than the increased written down value carried forward.

Partnerships

For partnerships commencing after 5 April 1994, the admission, death or retirement of a partner will no longer give rise to a notional cessation or commencement of the partnership. Provided that there is at least one partner common to the business before and after the change, the partnership will automatically continue. The commencement and cessation rules will instead apply to the individual partner who is joining or leaving the partnership, as in the following example:

Able and Bertie have been in partnership since 1 July 1994, making up their accounts to 30 June each year. On 1 July 1996 Carol joins the partnership.

Able and Bertie will automatically continue to be assessed on the current year basis on their share of the partnership profits as follows:

1996–97	Year ended 30 June 1996
1997–98	Year ended 30 June 1997

Carol will be treated as commencing on 1 July 1996, and will be assessed on her share of the partnership profits as follows:

1996–97	1 July 1996 to 5 April 1997
1997–98	Year ended 30 June 1997

She will therefore have overlap profits for the period 1 July 1996 to 5 April 1997.

For existing partnerships, the admission, death or retirement of a partner after 5 April 1994 will (up to 5 April 1997) result in a cessation and commencement, with the commencement being on the new current year basis. The partnership will, however, have the option as at present of electing under s113(2) ICTA 1988 to make a continuation election. The partnership would then continue to be assessed on the preceding year basis. Assuming instead that Able and Bertie commenced trading in 1980, the partnership assessments following the admission of Carol would be as follows on the basis that no continuation election is made:

Able and Bertie

1994–95	Year ended 30 June 1993 (PYB)
1995–96	Year ended 30 June 1994 (PYB)
1996–97	6 April 1996 to 30 June 1996

The Inland Revenue may amend 1994–95 and 1995–96 to the actual basis under s63 ICTA 1988.

Able, Bertie and Carol

1996–97	1 July 1996 to 5 April 1997
1997–98	Year ended 30 June 1997 (CYB)

All three partners would have overlap profits for the period 1 July 1996 to 5 April 1997.

Capital gains tax

Reinvestment relief

As discussed in the previous article, this relief is now extended so that *any* gain can be deferred by reinvesting it in the ordinary shares of a qualifying unquoted trading company. The one change from the detailed rules given in the previous article is that the exclusion of companies which hold more than half of their *chargeable* assets as land has been changed so that it is companies who hold more than half of their *total* assets as land that are excluded.

Important points concerning this relief are as follows:

a) It is only necessary to invest the amount of the *gain* in order to obtain full relief. Compare this to rollover relief where it is necessary to invest the amount of the *proceeds* in order to obtain full relief.

b) It applies before retirement relief, and so it may be necessary to claim less than the maximum possible relief in order that retirement relief is fully utilised. It is possible to claim reinvestment relief equivalent to the amount of the gain not covered by retirement relief, and there is therefore no wastage of retirement relief given at the rate of 50 per cent. This was not the case previously.

c) There is no reason why a person cannot re-invest in his or her own qualifying unquoted trading company. Therefore a person setting up or acquiring a qualifying unquoted trading company will be in a position to roll over, and thus postpone, any chargeable gains made within the previous three years.

d) It is not possible to claim both reinvestment relief and relief under the enterprise investment scheme in respect of the same shares.

Overseas activities

Foreign Income Dividend Scheme (FIDS)

As discussed in the previous article, companies with foreign source profits will from 1 July 1994 be able to pay a FID out of these profits. ACT is still payable on the FID, but any surplus ACT resulting from the payment of the FID is recoverable. The scheme will help companies with surplus ACT problems, but the drawback is that non-taxpaying shareholders will be unable to reclaim a tax credit. The following example demonstrates the advantages and disadvantages of the scheme:

For the year ended 31 March 1995 Bird plc has UK profits of £400,000 and overseas profits of £1,600,000. The overseas profits have been subject to overseas tax at the rate of 30%. On 15 March 1995 Bird plc paid a dividend of £1,000,000 to its shareholders, who are all non-taxpayers.

If the dividend is paid as a normal dividend the position is as follows:

	Total	*UK*	*Overseas*
	£	£	£
PCTCT	2,000,000	400,000	1,600,000
Corporation tax at 33%	660,000	132,000	528,000
Double taxation relief			
1,600,000 × 30%	(480,000)		(480,000)
	180,000	132,000	48,000
ACT	(128,000)		
MCT	52,000		

ACT paid is £250,000 (1,000,000 × 20/80), but the maximum set-off is:

UK profits 400,000 × 20%		80,000
Overseas profits – lower of:		
i) 1,600,000 × 20%	320,000	
ii)	48,000	48,000
		128,000

Bird plc therefore has surplus ACT of £122,000 (250,000 – 128,000) which it may not be able to utilise if this situation occurs on a regular basis. The surplus ACT of £122,000 therefore becomes an additional tax liability. The company's shareholders will receive gross income of £1,250,000 (1,000,000 + 250,000) as the related tax credit of £250,000 can be reclaimed.

Bird plc could have instead matched its dividend of £1,000,000 to its overseas profits of £1,600,000, and paid the dividend as a FID. It would still have paid ACT of £250,000 as normal, but would then have been able to reclaim its surplus ACT of £122,000. However, its shareholders would only have received gross income of £1,000,000, since a FID does not carry a tax credit as such.

In the case of taxpaying shareholders, the payment of a FID will leave them in exactly the same position as if a normal dividend had been paid. A company will therefore have to consider the tax status of its shareholders before opting for a FID. The first FID has in fact already been declared by BAT Industries plc, a company with high overseas earnings, and it increased the amount of its dividend by 25% to compensate non-taxpaying shareholders such as pension funds.

Personal finance

National Savings Pensioners Guaranteed Income Bond

The interest rate on the first issue of this bond is 7 per cent, and this is fixed for five years. The bond is aimed at providing a fixed monthly income for persons aged over 65. The maximum investment is £20,000 per person.

The Enterprise Investment Scheme

This scheme is aimed at providing equity finance for unquoted companies. Most of the rules covering the scheme were dealt with in the previous article, although some points warrant further consideration:

a) Qualifying companies

A qualifying company is one that is unquoted, trading in the UK, and carrying on a qualifying trade. There are a number of trades which do not qualify, such as leasing and banking. Property companies are specifically excluded

b) Qualifying investors

A qualifying investor is one who is liable to UK tax (whether or not he or she is resident in the UK) at the time the shares are issued, and who is not connected with the company. An investor is connected with a company if he or she is an employee of the company or (together with associates) holds over 30 per cent of the company's share capital. However, an investor can become a paid director at a later date without affecting his or her entitlement to the relief.

c) Withdrawal or relief

The relief will be withdrawn if:

i) the investor disposes of the shares within five years of their acquisition

ii) the company ceases to be a qualifying company within three years of the shares being issued

iii) the investor ceases to be a qualifying investor within five years of the shares being issued. This would be the case if the investor acquired more than 30% of the company's share capital

iv) the investor receives value from the company. For example, the company makes a loan or provides a benefit to the investor.

Relief is not withdrawn if the investor dies or the company is wound up for bona fide commercial reasons.

The full relief is withdrawn in all cases except where the investor disposes of the shares in an arm's length transaction. In this case the relief withdrawn will be limited to the disposal proceeds multiplied by the lower tax rate of 20 per cent, if this is less than the full relief.

The following example covers most of the main points:

Embryo Ltd is an expanding company owned by David Jones. The company requires additional finance to assist with its expansion plans, and David's brother Michael is going to invest £120,000 in a new issue of ordinary share capital on 30 June 1995. Michael, who is single, has taxable income of £50,000 p.a. He plans to join Embryo Ltd as a director within the next two years, and it is hoped that the company will obtain a listing on the stock exchange within the next four years. At this point Michael hopes to sell some of his shares for a substantial profit.

Michael will only qualify for relief on £100,000 of his investment, being the maximum relief available per tax year. If possible, he would therefore be advised to postpone at least £20,000 of his investment until after 5 April 1996. The relief will be £20,000 (100,000 at 20%), and this will be given as a credit against his tax liability. Michael's tax liability for 1995–96 is £16,295 as follows:

	£
3,000 at 20%	600
20,700 at 25%	5,175
26,300 at 40%	10,520
	16,295

The maximum relief for 1995–96 is therefore limited to Michael's tax liability of £16,295. However, as the investment has been made between 6 April and 5 October, Michael can carry back £3,000 (15,000 × 20%) of the relief to 1994–95. Since Michael can only obtain relief for £19,295 (16,295 + 3,000), he would be advised to invest £96,475 (19,295 × 100/20) on 30 June 1995, and to postpone the remaining investment of £23,525 (120,000 – 96,475) until after 5 April 1996.

Michael's future involvement as a paid director will not lead to the relief being withdrawn, but this will not be the case if Embryo Ltd obtains a stock exchange quotation before 30 June 1998 (within three years of the share issue). Even if Embryo Ltd obtains a stock exchange listing after 30 June 1998, Michael will still lose his relief on any shares sold before 30 June 2000 (within five years of the share issue). Provided that the shares are sold after this date the disposal will be exempt from CGT.

You should note that the rates and relief applicable to 1994–95 have been used in all of the examples in this article.

SECTION

8

UPDATES

Guidance notes

The following notes are based on the information provided by the Examiner at a meeting with teachers held at ACCA headquarters.

Balance of questions

Questions will be equally balanced between essay and computational questions. The emphasis in Paper 11 will be on providing advice supported by appropriate calculations.

Skills to be tested

A typical question will test students' ability to recall knowledge, to demonstrate an understanding of that knowledge and to apply that knowledge.

Paper 11 builds on the topics covered in Paper 7 Tax Framework, so a thorough understanding of the subject matter of Paper 7 is essential.

The only other paper which is relevant to Paper 11 is Paper 8 Managerial Finance, which includes a section on sources of finance. In Paper 11, the main emphasis of the section on sources of finance will be on the taxation implications of different sources of finance, although students would be expected to be aware of other factors which need to be considered in such as decision. There is no integration with any other papers in the Professional Stage.

The emphasis on CGT will be on business situations, and a question could require a student to consider the CGT and IHT implications of various gifts (of both business and non-business assets).

The area of personal finance can be summarised under three headings:

1 *Advising on the investment of clients' personal funds*

Sections 9(a), (b) and (e) of the syllabus have to be considered at the same time to make sense of the content. The current examinations have included questions on this area (e.g. Dec 1991 Q.5) but the new syllabus takes the subject a little further. Q.1 of the pilot paper indicates the depth required.

The factors which generally need to be considered are as follows:

i) the risk profile of a client;
ii) the client's tax position;
iii) the client's age and wealth;
iv) whether the investment is to be short, medium or long term;
v) whether the client is seeking income or capital growth (linked to their tax position);
vi) whether the investment is to be a lump sum or spread over a number of years.

2 *The regulations affecting financial advisers*

For the present the emphasis will be on the regulations as they affect accountants and only a 'broad' knowledge level would be expected. Q.1 of the pilot paper includes a typical example.

The detail given in the ACCA *Members' Guide to the Financial Services Act 1986* and the Association's Investment Business Rules is sufficient. With respect to other investment advisers, a broad knowledge of tied and untied agents will be sufficient.

3 The sources and costs of different forms of finance

This section interacts, to some extent, with Paper 8, although under personal finance, this will include small family companies raising finance. The emphasis will be on the taxation aspects of finance, although a knowledge will be required of the other factors that should be considered. The areas mentioned in the syllabus are:

Bank borrowing – overdrafts and short-, medium- and long-term loans.

Finance houses – hire purchase, leasing, and sale and leaseback arrangements.

Mortgages – both for unincorporated and corporate businesses.

Money and capital markets – share issues, loan capital, international borrowing such as Eurobonds, and venture capital for smaller companies.

A knowledge of taxation of exchange differences will not be examined.

Questions on the more complicated forms of finance such as convertible loan stock will not be set.

The taxation factors often do not differ that much between the different types of finance, that is, the differences between an overdraft and debentures would only warrant two or three marks.

The other factors which need to be considered would include:

i) the most appropriate finance in given circumstances, in other words, matching a long-term project to long-term finance;
ii) the effect on gearing;
iii) the effect on earnings per share (EPS);
iv) the legal factors, that is, borrowing limits;
v) the costs of servicing the finance, that is, interest rates.

These factors will be limited to a discussion and will not involve calculations (EPS or gearing). Q.6(d) of the pilot paper gives an example of the depth required.

Obvious examination areas would be a comparison of equity finance with loan finance or a comparison of buying an asset with leasing an asset.

Topics excluded from Paper 11

i) National insurance
The calculations of directors' NIC on a month by month basis.
For the purposes of class 4 NIC: the offset of trading losses against non-trading income.
Social security: the areas of benefit.

ii) Income tax
The pre-5 April 1990 rules for married couples.
Pre-5 April 1988 maintenance payments and deeds of covenant.
Relief for interest on home improvement loans.

8

The business expansion scheme.
Detailed computations in respect of share options, share incentives, profit sharing and profit related pay. An employee share ownership plan (ESOP) will not be examined in its own right.
A detailed knowledge of the conditions which must be met to obtain Inland Revenue approval for an occupational pension scheme.
Opening year losses relieved by aggregation.
The change of an accounting date.
A knowledge of first year allowances on plant and machinery acquired prior to 31 March 1986.
Agricultural buildings allowances prior to 1 April 1986.
Commercial woodlands.
The proposed abolition of the preceding year basis, and the introduction of self-assessment.

iii) Capital gains tax
The rules applicable to assets held on 6 April 1965.
The grant of a lease or sub-lease out of either a freehold, long lease or short lease.
The taxation of a company's capital gains prior to 17 March 1987.
A question would not be set in respect of the principal private residence where the taxpayer was not in occupation on 31 March 1982.
A detailed knowledge of the statements of practice on partnership capital gains.

iv) Inheritance tax
A detailed knowledge of gifts with reservation.

v) Trusts
Tax liabilities arising during a period of administration.
The 'tax pool' where insufficient 35% income tax has been paid by a discretionary trust.
The IHT aspects of discretionary trusts prior to 27 March 1974, and the situation where property is added to a discretionary trust.
Retirement relief.
The residence of trusts.
The overseas aspects of trusts.

vi) Value added tax
The special VAT schemes for retailers.
The capital goods scheme.
In respect of property and land; leases, do-it-yourself builders and demolition.
A detailed knowledge of penalties, apart from the default surcharge, serious misdeclarations and default interest.

vii) Corporation tax
Losses arising in accounting periods ending prior to 1 April 1991.
A detailed computational question on s.242 ICTA 1988 loss relief.
A detailed knowledge of the pay and file system.
A question will not be set on the interaction of consortium relief and group relief, although this does not preclude the situation where (a loss making) company has both a (profit making) 75% subsidiary and is also a consortium member (re a profit making consortium company).
The definition of a close company (although the consequences of being a close company are examinable).
Demergers and reconstructions (other than share-for-share amalgamations).

On discorporations, a question is unlikely to be set on the sale of a trade or business in return for shares. A question involving a double charge to CGT would not be set.

On liquidations, a question would not be set on the more complex areas such as the different types of liquidation, the preference of debts, or income and expenses arising during the liquidation. A question involving a double charge to CGT would not be set.

viii) Overseas activities

A detailed knowledge of double tax agreements.

ix) General

The names of cases or a detailed knowledge of the judgements are not required, although a knowledge of the principles derived from the leading cases *is* required.

A question will not be set requiring a knowledge of anti-avoidance legislation (that is, artificial transactions in land). However, a question might be set requiring comment as to the Inland Revenue's possible attitude towards a particular transaction/situation taking into account the principles from decided cases.

General approach to setting Paper 11

The approach to setting the paper will be as already outlined. Areas of current interest are likely to be examined; for example, particularly important decided case law such as *Pepper* v. *Hart*.

It is worth mentioning that some topics (such as overseas taxation) represent a disproportionate length of the syllabus. This is because the syllabus concentrates on those areas which are new to Paper 11.

Questions and Answers

Q *Would a question be set on the difference between operating in a business as a self-employed person or as a company and the effect of the employers' NIC on that?*

A Yes. Students will, therefore, need to know the rates of national insurance and whether the business is in or out of the SERPS scheme – it will not be simple Class 1 contributions.

Q *With respect to VAT, to what extent do students need to understand imports and exports particularly to the Single Market? This is asked in the context of the lead-in to Paper 11 where overseas aspects of taxation might feature the Single Market where VAT is very important. Are students expected to understand international services, reverse charges, groups, divisional registration, second-hand schemes?*

A As regards Paper 11, all these topics will be covered but second-hand schemes will require only a broad outline and retail schemes will not be covered.

Q *Will students need to know the requirements for having a pension scheme approved by the Inland Revenue?*

A Formal revenue approval for a company pension scheme will not be examined.

Q *Do students need to know the details of the sorts of benefits on retirement such as investment advice, AVCs and additional pension contributions?*

A Only broadly as now; for example, 25% can be a tax-free lump sum upon retirement and the rest of the pension will be taxable.

Q *As regards alternative treatments, for example, when Revenue Law is indistinct – a recent case being Schofield & Smith regarding pre-1965 assets, will either method be acceptable?*

A Where a point is in dispute, either method will be accepted.

Q *Will case studies become part of Paper 11 in due course?*

A Only in the form of mini case studies.

Q *With respect to loan interest and maintenance, is knowledge of pre-1988 rules required?*

A The transitional rules and the earlier rules are not examinable.

Q *How much corporate finance will be covered in the Paper 11 section on personal finance?*

A The coverage of corporate finance will be small – questions will look at the small family business as an extension of the individual, so it will not cover finance for larger companies such as plcs or multinationals.

Please remember to read the *Students' Newsletter* for information on any changes to the exam or the syllabus.

EXAM STYLE QUESTIONS

The best way to assess your progress is to practise for the examination by trying to tackle the types of question which you will meet in the examination room. This Section provides you with a selection of questions which illustrate the kind contained in the exam. They give representative coverage of the paper and are designed to help you practise answering questions in the different question formats which you will find in the exam paper itself. Try as many questions of this type as you can during your revision. You will find suggested answers in Section 12.

1

a) Owen MacDonald is 52 years old and has been a farmer for the past 20 years. He breeds pigs and grows winter wheat. Due to a poor harvest his accounts for the year ended 30 September 1994 show a tax adjusted loss of £8,500. His accounts included the following items:

i) Legal fees of £600 re a dispute over the boundary of a field.

ii) Amortisation of £800 in respect of a premium of £8,000 paid on 1 December 1993 for the ten year lease of a field.

iii) Compensation of £900 received for crops damaged when a convoy of travellers camped illegally on his land.

iv) Lease payments of £3,000 in respect of a motor car that was used entirely for business purposes. The car's original purchase price was £16,000.

v) An annual subscription of £48 to the *Pig Breeders' Gazette*.

Owen's written down value of plant and machinery at 6 April 1994 was £10,000, and there have been no additions or disposals during the past three years. Agricultural buildings allowance is claimed on items costing £12,000 in 1991. For the year ended 30 September 1993 Owen had a tax adjusted profit of £15,000. Owen has no other income, although he incurred a chargeable gain of £12,000 on 1 August 1994 when selling some shares. He is married to Olive, aged 47, who earns £6,000 p.a.

Required:

a) For each of the items (i) – (v) state what adjustment, if any, would have been made by the Inspector of Taxes in calculating Owen's tax adjusted loss.

b) After taking into account any advantageous claims, show Owen's tax position for both 1994/95 and 1995/96. Your answer should include the date by which any such claims will have to be made.

Relief should be taken for the loss as early as possible. All other claims should be made in such a way as to minimise the wastage of personal allowances. Owen has not previously made a claim for averaging of farmers profits. The tax rates and allowances for 1994/95 should be used throughout.

[16 marks]

b) Cindy is about to acquire shares in a publicly quoted company for £350,000 out of her own funds. The shares currently yield a dividend of £28,000 p.a. and the prospects of significant capital appreciation in the future are excellent. At the end of ten years Cindy may decide to sell some or all of the shares. It has been suggested to Cindy by a friend, Dominic, that instead of buying the shares herself she should form a new investment company, Cindy Ltd. Cindy would subscribe for 350,000 £1 shares in Cindy Ltd, which would then use the cash to buy the shares. Dominic has told Cindy that she could draw out director's remuneration of up to £10,000 p.a. and that Cindy Ltd could deduct this against the dividend income and that the balance of £18,000 would only be liable to the lower corporation tax rate of 25%. Dominic has said that Cindy could save tax on her director's earnings by paying premiums into a personal pension scheme.

Required:

c) Cindy has asked you whether the advice which she has received from Dominic is correct.

[9 marks]

[Total 25 marks]

2 Rudyard plc, a company which manufactures frozen desserts is reviewing its capital investment programme for the current accounts year ended 31 March 1995. It has asked you at today's date (which you should assume is 1 April 1994) to advise it on the potential tax implications of the proposed programme. Details are as follows:

a) The wall surrounding the company's factory premises in Manchester was condemned as unsafe on 1 January 1994. The wall will be replaced during the current year at a cost of £25,000. This cost will be provided for under the heading of repair expenditure in the accounts for the year ended 31 March 1994.

b) New factory premises are due to be constructed in Liverpool during the year. Production is due to commence on 31 July 1995. The company has not yet decided whether to buy the site outright for £400,000, including legal fees of £14,000, or to enter into a lease of the site at an annual rent of £60,000. The purchase or lease contract will be entered into in August 1994.

The costs of the building are estimated as follows:

	£
Architects' fees	30,000
Preparing the site	40,000
Construction	500,000
	570,000

It is proposed to enter into the building contract in November 1994. A government grant of £50,000 would be received towards the construction costs.

It is currently proposed that the expenditure on the factory premises should be allocated as follows:

Manufacturing processes	65%
Showrooms and shops	30%
Warehouse to store finished goods	5%
	100%

It may be possible, if advisable, to increase the expenditure devoted to the warehouse at the expense of the showroom.

c) Rudyard plc also operates a number of supermarkets. It is planning to open a new shop in Sheffield in March 1995. The cost of the freehold premises, which was previously in use as a restaurant, will be £140,000. This will be paid in October 1994. It is estimated that it will cost £25,000 to replace the roof, which is unsafe, and a further £43,000 to convert the premises into a supermarket. The sum of £43,000 is analysed as follows:

	£
Fixtures and fittings	19,000
Costs of securing fixtures permanently to premises	2,000
Suspended ceilings	8,000
Special lighting	2,000
Floor and wall tiles	5,000
Partitions	7,000
	43,000

The partitions would be used to separate the storage area permanently from the remainder of the shop.

d) It is planned to dispose of a supermarket in Leeds on 1 May 1994. The shop was acquired for £25,000 on 1 February 1975 and was extended at a cost of £12,000 on 1 May 1990. The market value at 31 March 1982 was £70,000. The company has decided not to elect that all of its assets should be regarded as having been acquired on 31 March 1982. The purchaser is anxious to obtain planning permission to demolish the shop and to use the land to build an office block. He has offered a sale price of either (i) £120,000 or (ii) £100,000 plus an extra sum equal to 10% of the value of the land after he has obtained planning permission (no extra sum would be paid if the purchaser fails to obtain planning permission).

Required:
Explain fully what you consider to be the correct tax treatments of the transactions described above, referring where appropriate to decided cases. Show all supporting calculations. Ignore VAT.

Assume the following RPIs:

March 1982	79.4
May 1990	126.2
May 1994	142.9

[Total 25 marks]

3 Mary, Mungo and Midge have been in partnership since 1983. They have asked for your taxation advice in respect of the following matters:

a) The partners share profits and losses in the ratio: Mary 55%, Mungo 20% and Midge 25%, after the payment of a salary of £10,000 to Midge. Midge has had to scale down his involvement with the partnership following a long illness, so on 1 January 1994, the profit sharing ratio was changed to: Mary 65%, Mungo 25% and Midge 10%. Midge also ceased to have a salary from that date.

In the accounts year ended 31 October 1993, the partnership made a tax adjusted loss of £24,000.

Required:
Show the allocation of the loss between the partners and outline their options for relieving their losses.

[8 marks]

b) Mary, who is single, has no other income apart from her partnership profits. Her share of the assessable profits for 1993/94 was £20,000 and for 1995/96 is expected to be £46,000.

Required:
Advise Mary whether she should claim relief under s380 or s385 taking both income tax and NIC considerations into account. Show all supporting calculations and assume that 1994/95 rates and allowances apply to all years.

[4 marks]

c) On 1 July 1994, Mary purchased some 12% government securities with a nominal value of £10,000. Interest is paid half-yearly on 30 June and 31 December. Mary sold the securities on 30 November 1994 for £11,000. The securities were purchased ex-div but were sold cum-div.

Required:
Advise Mary of the tax implications arising from her purchase and sale of these government securities.

[4 marks]

d) The partnership undertakes building work, all of which is standard rated. They seek advice regarding the completion of the VAT return for the quarter ended 31 July 1994. During this quarter the only contract was for an extension to a residential property. The work was commenced on 10 April 1994 and a progress payment of £5,000 was received on 1 June 1994. The work was completed on 28 July 1994. An invoice was issued for the total contract price of £12,000 plus VAT on 10 August 1994. The balance due, less a 5% retention, was received on 1 September 1994. During the quarter ended 31 July 1994, materials costing £3,000 (net of VAT) were purchased. £500 (net) of these were used by Mungo on his own house.

The partnership advises you that they have identified two errors on the previous quarter's return:

i) input tax was claimed in respect of entertaining costs of £170 (gross) and

ii) output tax was understated by £300.

The partnership pays in cash for all purchases, but does not operate the cash accounting scheme.

Required:

i) Explain the VAT rules relating to the time of supply for services.

ii) Show the entries to be made on the partnership's VAT return for the quarter ended 31 July 1994 in respect of this contract.

iii) Advise the partnership how they should treat the errors from the previous return.

iv) Explain how the partnership may benefit from joining the cash accounting scheme.

[9 marks]
[Total 25 marks]

4 a) You act as tax adviser to Robert Yates who is a widower aged 59 and who has been in business for twenty years as a sole trader, running a garage retailing petrol and repairing motor vehicles. Brian, his only child, is aged 29. Brian has been employed in the business for several years and is now anxious to take part in managing the business. Mr Yates proposes to make Brian a partner on 1 July 1994.

The recent tax adjusted profits of the business have been as follows:

	£
Year ended 30 June 1991	49,764
Year ended 30 June 1992	58,176
Year ended 30 June 1993	65,304
Year ended 30 June 1994	62,520

The profits for the year ended 30 June 1995 are expected to be £66,096.

Required:
Advise Mr Yates on the income tax and VAT implications of taking Brian into partnership. You should illustrate your answer with computations and assume that any favourable elections are made.

[12 marks]

b) Brian has been employed by the business for a number of years at an annual salary of £25,000. He anticipates earning considerably more than this once he becomes a partner. While an employee, Brian contributed 5% of his salary into the business's occupational pension scheme. As a partner, he plans to contribute a similar amount into a personal pension scheme. Brian has always used his own car for business purposes and has claimed capital allowances accordingly. This use of his car will still continue after he becomes a partner.

Required:
Advise both Brian and Mr Yates of the NIC implications resulting from the change in his status from an employee to a partner. Calculations of class 1 NIC liabilities are not required.

[6 marks]

c) Mr Yates has recently been in discussions with Paul Gold who owns Gold Ltd, a company manufacturing components for the motor industry. Gold Ltd is in need of new capital and proposes to issue some new ordinary shares. Mr Yates is considering subscribing for these shares and has heard that this investment may qualify for relief under the Enterprise Investment Scheme.

Required:
Advise Mr Yates of the conditions to be satisfied for the investment to qualify for relief under the Enterprise Investment Scheme. Your answer should cover:

i) the maximum that Mr Yates could subscribe and the way in which relief would be given

ii) the circumstances in which the relief could be withdrawn and how this withdrawal would be made

iii) whether it would be possible for Mr Yates to become a paid director of Gold Ltd.

[7 marks]

[Total 25 marks]

5 You act as tax adviser to Gary Barlow, a single man aged 43, who has traded for many years as an engineering contractor. A number of Mr Barlow's competitors have recently been made bankrupt and Mr Barlow (who owns a valuable private residence but no other non-business assets) has decided to incorporate his trade into a new company, Barlow Limited on 30 October 1994.

The following information is available:

a) *Adjusted trading profits:*

	£
Year ended 30 October 1990	13,000
1991	22,000
1992	29,000
1993	33,000
1994	38,000

The figure for the year to 30 October 1994 has been estimated without reference to the proposed incorporation.

b) *Capital allowances:*

Mr Barlow owned plant which as at 6 April 1991 had a written down value of

9

£8,000. No purchases or disposals of plant have taken place since then, other than the acquisition of a riveting machine for £3,000 on 1 February 1992. Maximum allowances have always been claimed. The open market value of the pooled assets at 30 October 1994 was £6,000; each asset had a market value and cost price below £6,000.

c) The summarised closing balance sheet of the business at 30 October 1994 is estimated to be as follows:

	£	£
Fixed assets		
Premises (at cost)	75,000	
Plant (NBV)	6,000	81,000
Current assets		
Stocks	4,000	
Debtors	2,500	
Cash at bank	1,400	
	7,900	
Less: Current liabilities		
Creditors	(6,400)	
Net Current assets		1,500
		82,500
Financed by:		
Capital account		52,500
Bank loan		30,000
		82,500

d) The business premises is currently valued at £100,000. It was acquired in December 1990.

e) The value of goodwill is currently estimated at £85,000. It had a nil value at 31 March 1982.

f) The company will acquire the stock at its market value of £9,000.

g) Mr Barlow has unused capital losses of £11,000 as at 6 April 1994. Of these £2,000 were incurred prior to 31 March 1982 and the remaining £9,000 were incurred in May 1984.

h) It has been agreed that the entire business (including cash) is to be incorporated in exchange partly for shares in Barlow Limited, the balance to remain outstanding on loan account. The amount of the loan is to be calculated so that it allows Mr Barlow to incur no CGT liability on the incorporation.

Required:

a) Advise Mr Barlow on the income tax, capital gains tax and VAT consequences of incorporating his business. Describe fully the conditions which must be met before any relevant reliefs may be claimed. Assume that the RPI for December 1990 is 129.9 and for October 1994 is 143.9.

[21 marks]

b) Mr Barlow does not have a mortgage, but he has undertaken other substantial financial commitments and wishes to draw out approximately £24,000 per annum from the company net of tax. He has asked you to advise him whether it would be a good idea for the company to pay him dividends as well as gradually repaying the loan.

[4 marks]

[Total 25 marks]

6 You are the tax adviser to Mr Tommy Cockles. Mr Cockles has recently incorporated a private company, Whelks Ltd, which has an issued share capital of 100,000 £1 ordinary shares, all of which are owned by Mr Cockles. Whelks Ltd will commence selling angling equipment to the general public in one month from today's date (which you should assume is 1 October 1994). Projected gross sales are £50,000 per month.

Mr Cockles has asked you for advice on the following matters:

a) On 1 September 1994 Whelks Ltd paid a sum of £3,000 in respect of a pre-launch advertising campaign. On the same date the company acquired a new car costing £10,000 and new office equipment costing £8,000. Mr Cockles is concerned that the company will not be able to obtain tax relief on any of this expenditure because the company was not trading at the time. He is also concerned that the company will not be able to recover any VAT element in these costs as it has not yet registered for VAT.

b) Mr Cockles also wants to know the time limits for registering for VAT and what would happen if the company were to register six weeks late in order to conserve its cash flow.

c) The premises of the company will be located in a newly designated Enterprise Zone. The cost of building the premises will be £120,000 (including £20,000 in respect of the land and £10,000 in respect of architect's fees). Mr Cockles wishes to confirm the tax consequences of acquiring these premises.

d) Mr Cockles is anxious to ensure that Nick Salmon, a senior manager with a multinational company, becomes the managing director of Whelks Ltd. Mr Salmon is reluctant to leave his current post and it has been suggested that either Whelks Ltd or alternatively Mr Cockles personally, should pay him £5,000 to join Whelks Ltd. Mr Cockles has asked for your comments, bearing in mind the potential tax implications for Mr Cockles, Mr Salmon and Whelks Ltd.

e) Assuming that Mr Salmon joins Whelks Ltd, it has been agreed that the company will provide him with a fixed entertainment allowance of £500 per month. Mr Cockles wishes to know what the tax (including VAT) implications of this arrangement might be for both Whelks Ltd and Mr Salmon.

f) Mr Cockles expects the company to expand rapidly in the future and foresees the need to issue further shares. Mr Mussel, who is a friend, has indicated his willingness to subscribe for a future issue of shares. In order to do so it will be necessary for him to take out a bank loan. He has asked Mr Cockles to find out whether the interest payable on such a loan will be eligible for tax relief.

Required:
Draft a memorandum dealing with each of the matters raised by Mr Cockles.

[Total 25 marks]

7 Jane and Christine each inherited a half share in a property on the death of their father in 1978. The probate value of the property was £80,000 and its market value as at 31 March 1982 was £70,000. The property was used as a holiday home. Neither of the sisters ever used the property as their main residence.

In May 1984, the sisters spent £8,000 on a new fitted kitchen and central heating.

In September 1994, a prospective purchaser offered £250,000 for the property. The sisters decided to accept this offer and contracts were exchanged in the same month. The legal fees in connection with the sale amounted to £4,000.

Jane is considering using part of her share of the sale proceeds to purchase shares in a manufacturing company run by a friend. She proposes investing the balance in investments producing tax-free income.

Christine intends to use her share of the sale proceeds as working capital for a new business venture which she will operate as a sole trader. Christine is currently a partner in a firm of solicitors. Her new venture, which she will initially undertake in the evenings and at weekends, is an interior design consultancy. The new venture will not involve any of the partnership's assets or staff.

Christine expects her income from the new business to be £20,000 per annum, net of VAT. All of her supplies will be standard rated and 75% of her customers will be VAT registered. The market for interior design is highly competitive and Christine believes that it will not be possible to pass the cost of VAT on to the 25% of her customers who are not VAT registered.

Christine will run her business from home, so her annual expenses will be minimal:

	£
Lease of photocopier	1,175
Telephone (50% private)	752
Entertaining	820
Insurance	625

Christine also plans to spend £3,525 on a pre-launch advertising campaign. All of the above figures are inclusive of VAT where applicable.

Required:

a) Calculate the capital gain arising on the sale of the holiday property.

Assume the following RPIs:

March 1982	79.4
May 1984	89.0
September 1994	143.8

The sisters have not made an election to have all gains computed by reference to March 1982 valuations. [4 marks]

b) Advise Jane of the conditions to be satisfied if she wishes to claim reinvestment relief. Your answer should cover:

i) the time limits within which the reinvestment must take place
ii) the amount she should invest in order to obtain the maximum relief
iii) the circumstances in which the gain will become chargeable. [5 marks]

c) Advise Jane which investments produce tax-free income. Your answer should specify the maximum that could be invested in each case. [6 marks]

d) Advise Christine:

i) whether she will automatically have to account for VAT on the income of her new business as a result of the partnership being registered for VAT
ii) assuming that the answer to (i) is that Christine will not automatically have to account for VAT, whether it would be beneficial for her to register voluntarily
iii) whether it would be beneficial for her to defer the pre-launch advertising expenditure until after she has commenced trading. Your answer should consider both the VAT and the income tax implications.

[10 marks]
[Total 25 marks]

8 Howard, born in 1926, has been running his own bookshop and mail order business since April 1975. The business is run through a company, Howdon Limited, in which Howard holds 5,000 £1 ordinary shares, the other 5,000 shares are held by his brother Donald. The shares were subscribed for at par in early April 1975.

9

In 1994, Howard decided to retire and in September agreed to sell his shares to Aardvark plc for £200,000, consisting of cash £150,000 and the issue of 12,500 shares in Aardvark plc valued at £4 each. The shares represent less than 1% of Aardvark's ordinary share capital.

Information regarding the assets of Howdon Limited is as follows:

	Cost	*Value at 31/3/82*	*Value at 30/9/94*
	£	£	£
Goodwill	Nil	25,000	100,000
Freehold premises	45,000	45,000	175,000
Shop fittings	21,000	20,000	44,000
Investment	3,000	5,000	16,000
Net current assets	15,000	25,000	65,000
		120,000	400,000

The fittings are moveable, each item cost less than, and at 30 September 1994 is worth less than, £6,000. The investment consists of 2,000 shares in ICI plc. The sale was completed on 30 September 1994.

It is now 1 March 1995. Howard proposes to make the following transfers:

- a gift of 2,500 shares in Aardvark plc to his daughter. The shares are now valued at £4.50 each
- a gift of £5,000 cash to Donald in consideration of his forthcoming marriage
- a gift of £2,000 cash to Oxfam, a recognised charity
- a settlement of £50,000 cash into a discretionary trust
- a loan of £20,000 cash to a friend at a market interest rate of 10% gross.

Howard has made only one earlier transfer: £120,000 into a discretionary trust on 1 April 1993. He is to pay any inheritance tax on the above transfers.

Howard's income for 1994/95 was £40,000. For 1995/96, apart from the interest he will receive from his friend, his only other income will be a pension of £200 per week, £750 (net) of building society interest, and a dividend of 8p per share from Aardvark plc, which is expected to be paid in May 1995.

Howard has been offered part-time employment as a consultant to Aardvark plc from 1 April 1995 at a salary of £600 per month. He is undecided whether to accept the offer.

Required:
Assume Howard is single and claims all available exemptions and reliefs.

a) Explain clearly using computations the tax consequences of the transaction carried out by Howard on 30 September 1994, and compute any capital gains tax payable.

b) Advise Howard of the consequences of his proposed transfers, including any steps he could take to minimise his liability.

c) Estimate the income tax that Howard will pay for 1995/96, showing clearly the additional income tax payable if he accepts the offer of part-time employment. Assume that 1994/95 tax rates and allowances continue to apply.

Assume the following RPIs:

March 1982	79.4
September 1994	143.8
March 1995	145.0

[Total 25 marks]

9

9 Robert Williams, a school teacher, inherited a site consisting of a hectare of land from his father in September 1992, when it had a probate value of £50,000. At that time he was advised that there was a prospect of land in the area being developed for commercial use at some time in the future. In the same month, Mr Williams signed a contract to acquire a further hectare of land adjoining the site which he had inherited. The second site cost £45,000 plus legal fees of £4,000, and in order to pay for it Mr Williams had to take out a loan of £30,000 on 1 November 1992. The loan carried a fixed interest rate of 10% p.a. and was repayable in ten years or on earlier sale of the property. No use was made of the land apart from occasional lettings to weekend campers.

In May 1993 Mr Williams obtained planning permission to build houses on both sites, subject to improvements being made to their drainage. In July 1993 he entered into a contract with a builder to carry out the necessary improvements for a price of £10,000. The work was completed and paid for in January 1994. All the land was sold to a property developer for £155,000 on 28 February 1994, and the loan was immediately repaid.

The following events then occurred:

3 June 1994: Mr Williams Inspector of Taxes raised a Schedule D Case I assessment for 1993/94 in respect of the disposal of the land, charging tax of £15,000.

1 July 1994: Mr Williams appealed against the assessment and applied to postpone tax of £2,000.

3 August 1994: the Inspector issued a notice agreeing to the postponement.

1 September 1994: Mr Williams paid the undisputed tax of £13,000.

1 January 1995: the General Commissioners heard Mr Williams' appeal against the assessment. They determined the appeal in favour of the Inspector and increased the tax charge to £16,800.

4 January 1995: the notice of determination of the appeal was issued to Mr Williams.

31 January 1995: Mr Williams paid the tax outstanding of £3,800.

Mr Williams' marginal rate of tax is 40%. He has made no other chargeable disposals during 1993/94.

Required:

a) Explain briefly the criteria employed by the courts to determine whether or not an isolated sale transaction constitutes an adventure in the nature of trade. [8 marks]

b) On the basis of (a) above, explain whether or not you would agree with the decision of the General Commissioners. [5 marks]

c) Calculate Mr Williams' tax liability on the disposal of the land (i) assuming that it is treated as a trading transaction, and (ii) assuming that it is treated as a capital transaction. Ignore any NIC implications. [6 marks]

d) Calculate any interest charges which Mr Williams may have incurred on late payment of tax. [6 marks]

Assume the following RPIs:

September 1992	139.4
July 1993	140.7
January 1994	142.0
February 1994	142.2

[Total 25 marks]

10 a) On 1 November 1993, Bob received a tax assessment on business profits for 1993/94, based on his return of income for the previous year. As he believed the assessment to be correct he did not appeal against it and paid the tax charged on the due dates.

Required:
Outline the circumstances under which (i) Bob and (ii) the Inspector dealing with Bob's case could obtain an alteration to the amount assessed at a later date. You should mention any relevant time limits which may apply.

[9 marks]

b) Paul made a chargeable capital gain of £18,000 in June 1994; disposal proceeds were £30,000. His brother Hugh made a chargeable capital gain of £2,600 in January 1995; disposal proceeds were £7,000.

Required:
i) Advise Paul of his responsibility for reporting his gain to his Inspector of Taxes:
   a) assuming that the Inspector issues a tax return in respect of 1994/95
   b) assuming that the Inspector does not issue a tax return in respect of 1994/95.

ii) Advise Hugh in the same way of his responsibility for reporting his gain:
   a) assuming that the Inspector issues a tax return in respect of 1994/95
   b) assuming that the Inspector does not issue a tax return in respect of 1994/95.

State briefly the penalties (other than interest charges) which may be imposed for failure to discharge these responsibilities. Assume that neither Paul nor Hugh are liable to income tax for 1994/95.

[9 marks]

c) Barney currently manufactures fitted kitchens for the general public from a small workshop. The market is highly competitive. He has a turnover of £40,000 p.a. which yields a current gross profit percentage of 40% and he incurs minimal overheads. He has been offered a contract to manufacture bookcases for a VAT registered trader at a price of £10,000 (exclusive of any VAT). Barney estimates that this project would involve a similar cost structure to his existing operations. Barney is concerned that, since he will become liable to register for VAT if he takes on the new contract, it may not be worthwhile to accept it. He has asked for calculations showing the net gain to him of taking on the contract. He has also enquired whether it would be possible to avoid the requirement to register by setting up a new company, Barney Ltd, to carry out the new contract.

Required:
Advise Barney on the best course of action with regard to the VAT.

[7 marks]
[Total 25 marks]

11 Leigh purchased a house in Kent, together with grounds of 1/2 hectare, on 1 May 1980 for £30,000. The value of the house at 31 March 1982 was £38,000. An extension was added at a cost of £12,000 in August 1985. Leigh occupied the house from 1 May 1980 until 30 September 1986. On 1 October 1986 she moved to live with her mother who was very ill. The house remained empty until 1 October 1988, from that date it was rented out until its sale for £140,000 on 30 June 1994.

Leigh also owns two other houses which are rented out unfurnished. The rent is due monthly in advance on 1 January, 1 February, etc. During 1994/95 the houses were let as follows:

House 1 was let on a landlord's repairing lease, at £4,800 p.a. The tenant left on 30 September 1994 owing four months rent. As the tenant is currently unemployed, Leigh realised that it was pointless trying to recover the outstanding rent. The house

9

was relet on 1 April 1995. Prior to reletting the house, Leigh had it redecorated at a cost of £1,500.

House 2 was purchased on 1 September 1994. On 3 September 1994, Leigh paid £2,000 to have structural repairs to a side wall. The house was let on a tenant's repairing lease at £4,200 p.a. from 1 December 1994.

Leigh also owns a furnished flat, which she rents out on a landlord's repairing lease, and from which she received rent of £4,680 during 1994/95. £1,300 of this rent can be considered as being in respect of the furniture. Leigh paid insurance of £400 during 1994/95, of which £150 was in respect of the building and £250 in respect of the contents.

Leigh also owns a leasehold shop. She acquired the ten year lease on 1 August 1993, paying a premium of £10,000. In addition she pays rent of £2,600 per annum. The rent is payable annually, in advance, on 1 August. The shop was empty until 1 May 1994 when Leigh sublet it unfurnished on a four year tenant's repairing lease. She charged a premium of £5,000 and an annual rent of £3,400 payable in advance.

Required:

a) Calculate the chargeable gain arising to Leigh in respect of the disposal of her Kent residence.

[7 marks]

b) After taking account of any advantageous claims, calculate Leigh's assessments under Schedule A and Schedule DVI for 1994/95.

[13 marks]

c) Leigh is considering furnishing her two houses and renting them out on a daily or weekly basis to tourists. She seeks your advice regarding:

   i) what conditions need to be satisfied for the tenancies to be treated as furnished holiday lettings

   ii) what taxation benefits this treatment will have.

Assume the following RPIs:

[5 marks]

March 1982	79.4
August 1985	94.8
June 1994	143.0

[Total 25 marks]

12 a) Charles Evans has been in business for five years retailing ladies' fashion. Charles is 56 years old and has recently been informed by his doctor that he is terminally ill. He is relatively unlikely to survive six years and is virtually certain to die within the next nine years.

Charles' sister Gabrielle has recently been made redundant. She has agreed to join Charles in the business. Charles is considering two possible proposals.

The first proposal would be to appoint Gabrielle as an employee on 6 April 1994. If he was still alive at that time, Charles would retire on 5 April 2000 and make a gift of the entire business to Gabrielle.

The second proposal would be to make an immediate gift of the entire business to Gabrielle. Charles would stay on as a partner sharing 50% of the profits, which would reflect the fair value of his contribution to the running of the business. He would, however, no longer have any interest in the assets of the business. Charles would again intend to retire on 5 April 2000.

The following information is also available:

i) Charles does not own any non-business assets, apart from his private residence which is valued at £140,000. This is not expected to increase greatly in value. Charles has left all his assets in his will to Gabrielle.

ii) Apart from net current assets of £58,000, the main asset of Charles' business is his shop which is currently valued at £240,000. One fifth of the shop has been let out for many years to a firm of accountants at a commercial rent. It is estimated that a sale of the entire shop would give rise to a chargeable gain of £40,000; however, further appreciation beyond the rate of inflation is most unlikely.

iii) The value of goodwill is currently negligible, but as profits are projected to rise it is expected to increase to £30,000 in the future.

iv) The tax written down values and market values of plant and machinery are both insignificant.

Required:
Advise Charles on the inheritance tax and capital gains tax implications for him and for his estate of the two alternative proposals. Outline briefly the main conditions which must be met before any relevant claims for relief can be made.

[15 marks]

b) Gabrielle expects to earn £20,000 per annum from her involvement with Charles' business. This will be her only source of income, as she has no savings. Gabrielle does, however, own jewellery worth £80,000 which she inherited on the death of her mother five years ago.

Gabrielle is married to Keith, who is employed as a computer programmer earning £40,000 per annum. Keith owns shares in quoted companies worth £50,000. These produce dividends of £2,500 (net) per annum. Keith also receives interest of £6,000 (net) per annum from building society deposits of £100,000.

The couple are the joint owners of a house valued at £150,000. There is an outstanding repayment mortgage of £50,000 (not under the MIRAS scheme) on which interest of £3,750 per annum is paid.

Gabrielle and Keith have both made wills which, upon the death of either of them, leave all their assets to the surviving spouse. They have two children aged 7 and 9.

Required:

i) Advise Gabrielle and Keith of tax planning measures that they could take in order to reduce their overall income tax liability for 1994/95 and future years. The couple do not wish to change their overall portfolio of investments.

ii) Advise Gabrielle and Keith of tax planning measures that they could take in order to reduce their potential inheritance tax liability. You should take into account the advice that you have already given in respect of income tax.

[10 marks]
[Total 25 marks]

13 Jimmy Corkhill and his wife Jackie, both aged 55, unfortunately died in a car crash on 5 October 1994. Jimmy was a director of Light plc, earning £4,000 per month, and also a partner in a firm of consultants. His share of profits for 1994/95 was £18,000. At the date of his death Jimmy owned the following assets:

a) His main residence valued at £290,000, which had been owned by his family for several generations.

b) A flat in London valued at £180,000 which was jointly owned with his wife. An endowment mortgage of £20,000 was secured on this property. The interest paid on the mortgage for the period 6 April 1994 to 5 October 1994 was £1,000 (gross).

c) Two shops valued at £75,000 each, and each rented out at £8,000 pa. The rent was payable quarterly in advance (1 January, 1 April etc), with the tenants responsible for repairs. However, one shop was unlet from 1 July 1994 to 5 October 1994, and during this period had been decorated at a cost of £900.

d) A villa in Konghow which had cost 100,000 Konghowan dollars when the exchange rate was $2 to £1. Its value has not changed but the exchange rate on 5 October 1994 was $4 to £1. Konghowan inheritance tax of $15,000 is payable in respect of the villa as a result of Jimmy's death.

e) A quarter share of the partnership assets which are valued at £400,000. The partners have signed an agreement whereby upon a partner's death the other partners are obliged to buy, and the personal representatives of that partner are obliged to sell, that partner's share of the assets.

f) 20,000 shares in Light plc. The shares were quoted at 192 – 196 on 5 October 1994, with bargains on that day of 190, 195 and 199. A dividend of 6p per share was paid on 31 August 1994. Light plc only pays one dividend per year which is always on 31 August.

g) 2,000 units in the Rapide unit trust, valued at 110 – 115.

The joint funeral expenses came to £3,000. Jimmy was also a beneficiary of two trusts:

i) Under a trust set up by his uncle to hold 30,000 shares in Light plc, he was entitled to all the income after the payment of an annuity of £1,500 (gross) to his sister. The annuity was paid monthly, at the end of each month.

ii) Under a trust set up by his grandfather to hold assets worth £30,000 he was one of the beneficiaries who could receive the income at the trustees' discretion. On 1 October 1994 he had received a payment from the trust of £1,625, which represented the entire trust income for the past six months.

Jimmy's brother Billy is the sole beneficiary of Jimmy's estate. The executors sold the flat for £160,000 on 1 December 1994, and the villa in Konghow on 1 February 1995 for $100,000 when the exchange rate was $5 to £1. The administration of the estate was completed on 31 July 1995, and the remaining assets passed to Billy. He then sold one of the shops for £80,000 on 1 August 1995.

Required:

a) Calculate Jimmy's statutory total income for 1994/95.

[6 marks]

b) Calculate the IHT that will be payable as a result of Jimmy's death. Show who is liable for the tax and by what date. You should assume that Jimmy's income tax liability for 1994/95 was £9,000, and ignore the disposals of property that occurred after the date of Jimmy's death.

[13 marks]

The gross dividend yield on the FT actuaries all-share index should be taken as 5%. You should assume that the Inland Revenue base their valuation of an interest in a trust on the trust income of the previous twelve months.

c) i) State whether it would be beneficial for the executors to make a claim in respect of land and buildings sold after death.

ii) Billy is concerned about his future IHT liability should he and his wife both die within the next few years. He was already wealthy before his inheritance, and has two young children. State what Billy could do in order to mitigate this possible future IHT liability.

[6 marks]
[Total 25 marks]

14 Edna Brader is 65 years old. In May 1994, Edna decided to transfer quoted shares in Capinch plc, a multinational company, into a trust for her grandchildren. All of the grandchildren are under 16 years of age. The shares are valued at £200,000 and the transfer will realise a capital gain of £40,000.

Edna is unsure whether the trust should be an accumulation and maintenance trust or a discretionary trust. She has made no previous transfers and will pay any taxes or costs associated with setting up the trust.

Edna's daughter Carol got married in October 1994. Edna gave her an antique clock worth £7,500 as a wedding present. Edna had inherited the clock on the death of her sister in July 1986 when it was valued at £2,500. The clock is not heritage property.

Edna also wishes to make a gift of agricultural land and buildings to her brother Nelson. Edna purchased the land in March 1983 for £50,000. The land has always been let out to tenants and the current tenancy agreement is due to come to an end in December 1994. The land is currently valued at £120,000 for agricultural purposes, but Edna is seeking planning permission which will increase the value to £200,000. Nelson already owns the neighbouring land, and its value is expected to increase by £30,000 as a result of the gift.

Required:

a) Explain the current and potential CGT and IHT implications for Edna of setting up (i) an accumulation and maintenance trust and (ii) a discretionary trust. (**Note:** you do not have to consider the tax implications for the trusts themselves.)

[8 marks]

b) Explain the CGT and IHT implications of all of the trust property being distributed to the grandchildren in five years time, assuming that the trust is (i) an accumulation and maintenance trust and (ii) a discretionary trust. Assume that the beneficiaries will meet any IHT due.

[8 marks]

c) Explain the CGT and IHT implications of the gifts to Carol and Nelson. In respect of the gift to Nelson, assume that Edna obtains planning permission and makes the gift in December 1994.

[9 marks]

Assume the following RPIs:

March 1983	83.1
July 1986	97.5
October 1994	143.9
December 1994	144.4

[Total 25 marks]

15 You are the tax adviser to Jones Ltd, a UK resident company, that for many years has been manufacturing confectionery. In recent years, however, the company's confectionery business has been in decline and it has now decided to cease this business at the end of its current accounting year on 31 December 1994. The company then plans to continue in business by setting up a chain of warehouses retailing confectionery and soft drinks. It expects to make a tax adjusted schedule D1 trading loss of £250,000 in the current year which is entirely in respect of the confectionery business. You have the following information on Jones Ltd:

9

a) The tax adjusted schedule D1 trading profits for recent periods have been:

	£
12 months to 30 September 1990	14,000
12 months to 30 September 1991	57,000
12 months to 30 September 1992	45,000
3 months to 31 December 1992	7,000
12 months to 31 December 1993	30,000

b) Rental income of £6,000 per quarter is received in respect of one floor of the company's office building which is rented out. The rental commenced on 1 October 1991.

c) On 1 February 1991 the company made a chargeable gain of £11,000 when disposing of some investments.

d) The company issued £160,000 of 12% debentures on 1 April 1991, with interest due on 31 March and 30 September each year. These are not redeemable until 2004.

e) A ten year deed of covenant to charity for £6,000 p.a. (gross) was entered into in 1987, with payment being made on 1 October each year.

f) Dividends paid during recent periods have been:

	£
12 months to 30 September 1990	15,000
12 months to 30 September 1991	7,500
12 months to 30 September 1992	7,500
3 months to 31 December 1992	Nil
12 months to 31 December 1993	Nil

No dividend is to be paid in respect of the current year.

g) The company has two subsidiaries, Tom Ltd which owns several restaurants, and Jerry Ltd which runs a printing business.

i) Tom Ltd became a subsidiary on 1 January 1993 when Jones Ltd acquired 60% of its share capital. Tom Ltd has always had an accounting date of 31 December, and regularly makes annual profits for tax purposes of £20,000. The other 40% of Tom Ltd's share capital is held by Minor Ltd, an unconnected UK resident company.

ii) Jerry Ltd became a subsidiary on 1 April 1994 when Jones Ltd acquired 70% of its share capital. The remaining 30% of Jerry Ltd's share capital was already held by Tom Ltd, who acquired its holding on 1 April 1992. Jerry Ltd has always had an accounting date of 31 March, and regularly makes annual profits for tax purposes of £10,000.

Neither Tom Ltd nor Jerry Ltd has paid a dividend in recent years, and both are UK resident.

h) Jones Ltd has a holding of 250,000 £1 ordinary shares in Multi PLC, a UK quoted company, which was acquired in 1986. Multi Ltd regularly pays a dividend of 6 pence per share which is received on 1 January each year. Jones Ltd's holding in Multi PLC represents less than 5% of that company's share capital.

Required:
Draft a memorandum to the directors of Jones Ltd explaining the alternative ways in which their company will be able to obtain relief for its expected loss of £250,000 for the year ended 31 December 1994. Your memorandum should include the maximum amount that can be claimed under each alternative, and the date by which each relief should be claimed. You should ignore the possibility of any repayment supplement being due to Jones Ltd.

[Total 25 marks]

16 Apricot Ltd has been trading for many years. However, owing to deteriorating results, it has decided to cease trading on 30 September 1994 (which you should assume is one month from today's date).

The forecast profit and loss account for the six months to 30 September 1994 is as follows:

	£	£
Gross profit		120,500
Less:		
Allowable administration expenses	122,500	
Depreciation	16,000	
Debenture interest paid (gross)	5,000	
Charitable deed of covenant (gross)	1,000	
Redundancy payments	50,000	
Professional fees	2,000	
		(196,500)
Net loss		(76,000)

The following information is also available:

The debenture interest is paid wholly and exclusively for the purpose of Apricot Ltd's trade.

The redundancy payments are in respect of Apricot Ltd's five employees. Each employee is to be paid £10,000, which includes their statutory payment of £2,000 each.

The professional fees relate to advice on the proposed cessation of trading.

On 30 September 1994 the company's assets will be sold for their open market values. This sale will result in capital losses of £15,000 and balancing allowances of £45,000.

Apricot Ltd was incorporated on 1 April 1990. Its results since incorporation have been as follows:

Year ended	31/3/91	31/3/92	31/3/93	31/3/94
	£	£	£	£
DI profits	60,000	26,000	29,000	7,000
Capital gains	–	19,000	–	–
Capital losses	8,000	–	–	–
Debenture interest paid	10,000	10,000	10,000	10,000
Charitable deed of covenent paid	1,000	1,000	1,000	1,000
Dividends paid (net)	15,000	7,500	–	–

The figures given above in respect of the debenture interest and the charitable deed are gross.

The share capital of Apricot Ltd is owned as follows:

Melon Ltd	40%
Plum Ltd	40%

None of the other shareholders owns in excess of 5% of the share capital.

The forecast results of Melon Ltd and Plum Ltd for the year ended 31 March 1995 are as follows:

	Melon Ltd	Plum Ltd
	£	£
Tax adjusted profit/(loss)	110,000	(8,000)
Schedule D III income	10,000	–
Trade charges (gross)	(30,000)	–

Both companies subscribed for their shareholdings on the date of Apricot Ltd's incorporation, each paying £40,000. After repaying creditors and debenture holders, Apricot Ltd expects to have liquidation proceeds of £150,000 available to distribute to its shareholders. This distribution is expected to take place in December 1994.

Melon Ltd and Plum Ltd are not connected to each other, and neither of them has any other shareholdings. Both they and Apricot Ltd are resident in the UK.

Required:

a) Compute the corporation tax payable by Apricot Ltd for all of its accounting periods. Your answer should include details of any tax refunds due, and any losses or charges that are unrelieved. You should ignore the possibility of any repayment supplement being due.

[13 marks]

b) Compute the tax liabilities of both Melon Ltd and Plum Ltd for the year ended 31 March 1995.
Assume the following RPIs:

April 1990	125.1
December 1994	144.4

[8 marks]

c) Briefly discuss the consequences of Apricot Ltd declaring a dividend prior to the cessation of its trade.

[4 marks]
[Total 25 marks]

17 H Ltd owns 76% of the ordinary share capital of A Ltd and 40% of the ordinary share capital of D Ltd. The remaining ordinary shares in A Ltd are owned by individual members of the general public. The remaining ordinary shares in D Ltd are owned equally by P Ltd and Q Ltd, both of which are unconnected with H Ltd or with each other. A Ltd owns 80% of the ordinary share capital of B Ltd which in turn owns 75% of the ordinary share capital of C Ltd. H Ltd owns 5% of the ordinary shares in B Ltd and 0.1% of the ordinary shares in C Ltd. The remaining ordinary shares in B Ltd and C Ltd are owned by individual members of the general public. All of the companies concerned are trading companies resident in the UK. The issued share capital of each company consists of ordinary shares only.

Required:

a) i) State, giving reasons, which set (or sets) of the above companies form a group (or groups) for capital gains tax purposes.

ii) Describe the general tax treatment of a transfer of an asset from one group company to another where the asset was a fixed asset of the first company but forms part of the trading stock of the second company.

iii) Describe the second company's right of election in these circumstances and indicate when such an election would be likely to be favourable.

[9 marks]

b) i) State, giving reasons, which of the above companies can surrender trading losses to other companies, in each case identifying those other companies concerned.

ii) Explain the rules regulating the amount of the loss which can be surrendered in each case.

iii) Would your answer to (b) (i) have been different if firstly Q Ltd was not resident in the UK or secondly A Ltd was not resident in the UK?

[9 marks]

c) i) State, giving reasons, which of the above companies can elect to pay dividends to other companies without accounting for ACT.

ii) Explain the possible benefits of such an election.

[7 marks]
[Total 25 marks]

18 Grudge Ltd is the parent company of a group which includes its three wholly owned manufacturing subsidiaries, Envy Ltd, Ire Ltd and Poison Ltd. The shares in Grudge Ltd are owned equally by Dr Choler (the managing director of Grudge Ltd), Mr Borgia and Miss Nightshade. Envy Ltd has made trading losses in recent years as a result of excessive staffing levels. The group has had insufficient funds to finance the necessary redundancies in Envy Ltd which are estimated to cost £210,000. Dr Choler is considering purchasing Envy Ltd on 1 July 1994. The following additional information is available:

a) Dr Choler would acquire the shares in Envy Ltd for £200,000. Their current market value is estimated to be £250,000.

b) Dr Choler would subsequently subscribe £210,000 for a further issue of shares in Envy Ltd. This would provide the company with sufficient funds to finance the redundancy programme.

c) Dr Choler would borrow £100,000 from a UK bank to assist him in acquiring his shares in Envy Ltd. The balance of £310,000 would come from his own resources.

d) Dr Choler intends to finance his loan repayments and associated interest costs out of personal loans made to him by Envy Ltd.

e) Dr Choler would not be actively engaged in the management of Envy Ltd, although he would continue to act as managing director of Grudge Ltd at a salary of £95,000 p.a. He has no other income apart from this salary.

f) Dr Choler wishes to know if he can obtain income tax relief for his interest costs.

g) Grudge Ltd had acquired the shares in Envy Ltd for £40,000 on 6 April 1970. The value of the shares on 31 March 1982 was £100,000. Grudge Ltd held no other assets at 31 March 1982.

h) After Envy Ltd has been acquired by Dr Choler, it will immediately implement the redundancy programme. Dr Choler wishes to know if any expenditure will be allowable for corporation tax purposes.

i) Envy Ltd currently has unused trading losses of £300,000. Dr Choler wishes to know if these will be available to set against future trading profits of the company.

j) In August 1989 Envy Ltd had transferred buildings to Ire Ltd at their then market value of £80,000. The buildings had cost Envy Ltd £60,000 in November 1984.

Required:

a) Explain the potential tax implications arising on the proposed sale of Envy Ltd for (i) Dr Choler; (ii) Envy Ltd; and (iii) the other companies in the Grudge Ltd group. Assume that the RPI for March 1982 is 79.44 and for July 1994 is 143.5.

[21 marks]

b) Grudge Ltd and its subsidiaries have been registered as a group for VAT purposes. None of the group companies make exempt supplies but Envy Ltd exports 90% of its production, with the remaining 10% being sold to other group members.

Describe the VAT implications for Envy Ltd of leaving the Grudge Ltd group.

[4 marks]
[Total 25 marks]

19 You act as tax adviser for Bliss Ltd (which operates a successful marriage bureau) and its managing director, Mr Crippen. The company has made tax-adjusted trading profits of £200,000 p.a. over the previous five years. It has now built up a substantial reserve of cash, since its policy has been not to pay out any dividends. The company has not made any chargeable gains in recent years and has always made up its accounts to 31 March. Mr Crippen informs you that he and Mr Bluebeard, his fellow shareholder, are in serious disagreement about the future strategy of the company and that this is having a very harmful effect on the running of the business. It has therefore been decided that Mr Bluebeard should no longer be involved in the management of the company and that the company should purchase all of his shares back from him.

Further relevant information is as follows:

a) Mr Bluebeard is 66 years old and has worked in the company as a full-time director since it was incorporated on 1 February 1986. He acquired 30% of the ordinary shares in Bliss Ltd at par on 1 February 1986 for £30,000.

b) Mr Bluebeard, who is single, has a private income of £40,000 p.a. He has made no disposals of assets since 6 April 1988.

c) The company has agreed to buy back Mr Bluebeard's shareholding at its market value of £600,000 on 1 February 1995.

d) All of Bliss Ltd's assets are in use for the purpose of its trade.

Required:

a) Outline the main conditions which must be met before a company's purchase of its own shares qualifies for the special treatment introduced by the Finance Act 1982. Do not consider any provisions relating specifically to groups of companies.

[6 marks]

b) Set out the amount and timing of the tax liabilities which would be incurred by both Mr Bluebeard and Bliss Ltd in respect of the share purchase, on the assumption that:

i) The purchase does not qualify for the special treatment;
ii) The purchase does qualify for the special treatment.

Explain fully the basis for the differences between the two calculations and state briefly the qualifying conditions for any relief claimed.

[17 marks]

c) State the circumstances in which Bliss Ltd might become entitled to repayment supplement.

[2 marks]

Assume the following RPIs:

February 1986	96.6
February 1995	144.9

[Total 25 marks]

20 Octopus Ltd, a UK resident company, manufactures motorcycles. The directors seek your advice concerning the following taxation matters:

a) During its accounts year ended 31 March 1995, Octopus Ltd made a trading profit of £1,600,000. In addition it received a dividend of £6,300 (net of 10% withholding tax) from Dolmus Inc, a company resident in Dolmania. Octopus Ltd owns 15% of the ordinary share capital of Dolmus Inc, and is the only foreign shareholder. Dolmus Inc pays Dolmanian corporation tax at the rate of 30%. During the accounts year ended 31 March 1995, Octopus Ltd paid debenture interest of £30,000 and a dividend of £465,000. At 1 April 1994, Octopus Ltd had surplus ACT brought forward of £200,000.

Required:
Calculate Octopus Ltd's mainstream corporation tax for the year ended 31 March 1995.

[8 marks]

b) For several years now, Octopus Ltd has been exporting its motorcycles to the country of Rubeenia. Octopus Ltd is now planning to set up a permanent business establishment in Rubeenia to assist with these sales and to handle the subsequent repair and servicing work. It is proposing to open the new establishment on 1 April 1995. Corporation tax rates in Rubeenia are approximately 80% of the corresponding UK rates.

Required:
Explain the taxation consequences of setting up the establishment in Rubeenia as (i) a branch and (ii) a wholly owned subsidiary. Your answer should deal specifically with the following points that have been raised by the directors:

1) The possibility of the Rubeenian establishment making a trading loss in its initial years of trading.
2) The effect of Octopus Ltd selling goods to the Rubeenian establishment at an undervalue.
3) The purchase of equipment by the Rubeenian establishment for servicing the motorcycles.
4) Whether there would be taxation benefits from delaying remittances of distributable profits to the UK until after the end of the year to which they relate.

[9 marks]

c) Assume that Octopus Ltd decides to set up a subsidiary which is regarded as resident in Rubeenia and that the rate of Rubeenian corporation tax is reduced to 60% of the corresponding UK rate.

Required:
i) Explain whether or not the Rubeenian subsidiary will be classed as a controlled foreign company.
ii) Explain the consequences of being classed as a controlled foreign company.
iii) Explain how these consequences can be avoided.

[5 marks]

d) Frank Squid is a director of Octopus Ltd. He is Rubeenian but has been living and working in the UK since 1 May 1993. During 1994/95 he earned a salary of £45,000 from Octopus Ltd. Most of his duties are undertaken in the UK, however he spent three months of the year visiting Rubeenia in order to acquire a site and hire staff for the new Rubeenian establishment. Frank's contract with Octopus Ltd is for a period of five years, at the end of this period he proposes to return to Rubeenia. Frank has a bank account in Rubeenia which was credited with gross interest of £6,000 (sterling equivalent) during 1994/95. Frank withdrew £2,000 of this interest while he was in Rubeenia, in order to fund his spending over there. He brought £500 back with him into the UK.

Required:
Outline Frank Squid's residence, ordinary residence and domicile status and explain the basis on which his 1994/95 income will be assessed. You are not required to compute his income tax liability.

[4 marks]

[Total 25 marks]

21 Mark Owen is British. He is 25 years old, single, and has lived in the UK since birth. On 31 July 1994, he moved to Australia to take up employment as a television presenter. His contract is initially for five years, but will almost certainly be renewed if the programme is successful.

Mark owns a house in Oldham, which is being purchased with the aid of a £40,000 mortgage. He proposes to rent out his house while he is abroad and has appointed a UK agent to arrange a long lease and to manage the letting.

Mark owns some shares in UK quoted companies and some UK government securities. Mark proposes to purchase a house overseas once he is established in his new job, and will probably sell some of his UK investments in order to raise the necessary finance.

Mark's sister and his parents will remain in the UK and he intends to spend his annual six week vacation visiting them. Once his contract is finally terminated he proposes to return permanently to the UK.

Required:

a) Advise Mark whether he will:

   i) be treated as resident and/or ordinarily resident in the UK for 1994/95 onwards, and

   ii) remain within the scope of UK inheritance tax.

[7 marks]

b) Explain Mark's income tax position on both UK and overseas sources of income while he is abroad.

[5 marks]

c) Explain Mark's capital gains tax and inheritance tax position on both UK and overseas assets:

   i) whilst he is living and working abroad, and

   ii) on his eventual return to the UK.

[5 marks]

In all cases your answer should cover any tax planning points that Mark should consider while he is abroad. You should confine your answer to his UK tax position.

d) Tabitha is resident, ordinarily resident and domiciled in the UK. Tabitha's employer, Genie plc, has recently offered her the chance of a secondment to the company's new offices in Tokyo. The secondment will commence on 1 September 1994 and end on 30 September 1995. Tabitha will be permitted two months' leave during the period of the contract. This leave must be taken during November 1994 and March 1995. In addition to her salary, Genie plc will pay for all travelling and accommodation.

Required:

Explain Tabitha's potential liability to UK taxation whilst she is working overseas. In particular, you should advise her whether or not it would be beneficial for her to remain outside the UK during her two months' leave.

[8 marks]

[Total 25 marks]

22 Derek and Phoebe Myers have been married for six years. Derek was employed as a bank clerk with the Barminster Bank but, owing to rationalisation in the banking industry, he was made redundant on 30 April 1994. On that date, the bank paid him his final month's salary of £1,500 plus a lump sum of £40,000. £15,000 of this sum was his statutory redundancy entitlement, the balance was an ex-gratia payment.

Derek has always taken a keen interest in financial matters. He has made a success of investing modest sums of his own money in the stock market and has therefore decided to set up in business as an investment adviser.

Phoebe is the personnel director of Quest plc, an electronics company. She earns £35,000 per annum. She currently contributes 6% of her salary to her employer's occupational pension scheme.

On 1 June 1994, Quest plc issued 3,000 £1 ordinary shares to each of its directors. Phoebe paid the par value for these shares, although their market value at 1 June 1994 was £4. On the same date, each director was also given the option to buy a further 5,000 shares at their value as at 1 June 1994, less a discount of 30%. The options were provided free and must be exercised within three years of their issue. The ordinary shares of Quest plc are forecast to be worth £10 by 31 May 1997.

Quest plc has provided Phoebe with a new 1800cc diesel powered motor car at a cost of £18,800. Subsequent to its purchase, the car was fitted with a mobile telephone costing £705, and this was invoiced for separately to the purchase of the motor car. Both figures are inclusive of VAT. Phoebe drives less than 2,500 business miles a year, and private fuel and telephone calls are paid for by Quest plc.

Required:

a) Outline to Derek the provisions of the Financial Services Act 1986 governing the need to be authorised to conduct investment activities. Your answer should cover:

   i) who is responsible for authorising advisers
   ii) what type of activities need to be authorised
   iii) what types of investment can be undertaken without authorisation.

[7 marks]

b) Explain to Phoebe what steps she could take to increase the benefits which she will receive on retirement. Identify the maximum amount which she could invest and explain how this sum will be treated for tax purposes.

[5 marks]

c) Explain the income tax implications arising from:

   i) the termination payment received by Derek, and
   ii) the provision of the shares and the share option in Quest plc received by Phoebe.

[6 marks]

d) i) Explain the income tax and NIC implications for Phoebe arising from the provision of the car and mobile telephone.

   ii) Explain the corporation tax, NIC and VAT implications for Quest plc arising from the provision of the car and mobile telephone.

[6 marks]
[Total 25 marks]

Answers to Section 9 begin on page 81.

SECTION

10

PILOT PAPER QUESTIONS

The following pilot paper has been written by the examiner to give you some idea of the style and format of the examination under the new syllabus. The pilot paper gives you a chance to test your understanding of much of the course material. It also provides an opportunity to attempt a full paper under exam conditions, that is, without referring to your notes, and limiting yourself to the time allowed for the exam itself. You will find advice on how you should have answered each question in Section 13.

Time allowed – 3 hours

Number of questions on paper – 6

FOUR questions ONLY to be answered

Tax rates and allowances are on pages 3–5.

1 You are a qualified Certified Accountant in part-time private practice, although you are not authorised to conduct investment business under the Financial Services Act 1986. A friend of yours, George Hope, and his sister Mildred have recently inherited £25,000 each, which they wish to invest. George is aged 42, single, and is presently paying income tax at the rate of 40%. He plans to set up as a self-employed builder in two or three years' time, at which date he will require all of the £25,000 as start-up capital. Mildred is aged 37, and is also single. She presently pays income tax at the rate of 25%, and has no requirement for the £25,000 in the foreseeable future. She is, however, reluctant to invest the money in anything that is of a 'risky nature'. They have asked for your advice in respect of three possible investments, which are:

i) Personal equity plans
ii) Government stocks
iii) TESSAs.

George and Mildred have also asked you to select the appropriate investments for them, for example which personal pension plan or which TESSA. Because George is a friend of yours, you are not going to charge him for your investment advice, but Mildred is to be charged your normal fee.

Required:

a) i) Briefly define the term 'investment activity' for the purposes of the Financial Services Act 1986.

ii) Which of the three possible investments are within the definition of 'investments' for the purposes of the Financial Services Act 1986?

iii) State whether you would need to be authorised to conduct investment business under the Financial Services Act 1986 in order to provide your advice to George and Mildred.

[10 marks]

b) For each of the three possible investments:

i) Set out the potential implications for George and Mildred in respect of income tax and CGT. Your answer should include a brief description of each type of investment and, where relevant, details of the maximum amount that can be invested under each option.

ii) Advise George and Mildred as to the suitability of each of the three possible investments to their particular financial requirements. You are not to consider any other possible investments.

[15 marks]
[Total 25 marks]

2 Peter Jones is 80 years old and, due to ill health, is not expected to live beyond the next three months. The value of his estate as at 1 December 1994, and a forecast value in 12 months time, is as follows:

	Value at 1.12.94 £	*Forecast value* £
10,000 shares (a 2% holding) in Bluechip PLC a quoted company	40,000	36,000
4,000 shares (a 1% holding) in Giltedge PLC, a quoted company	60,000	75,000
20,000 shares (an 8% holding) in Nobody Ltd, an unquoted company	45,000	40,000
Private residence	200,000	220,000
Holiday home	120,000	105,000
	465,000	476,000

Peter has owned all of these assets for at least two years. Under his will, Peter has left all of his assets to his two daughters, Susan and Jenny. Both Susan and Jenny have children. Peter's wife is also ill, and is not expected to live much longer than him. She has no assets of her own, but he is confident that his daughters will look after her upon his death.

Peter has made the following transfers of value during his lifetime:

i) On 1 August 1986, he made a gift of £100,000 into a discretionary trust, with all taxes being paid by the trust.

ii) On 1 September 1991, he gave Susan £90,000 as a wedding gift.

iii) On 1 October 1991, he gave Jenny his estate agency business which was valued at £200,000. Peter had run the business for 15 years prior to that date, and Jenny has continued to run it since.

Required:

a) Calculate the inheritance tax liabilities that would arise if Peter were to die on 1 December 1994.

[8 marks]

b) Discuss the possible inheritance tax benefits that could be obtained as a result of changing the provisions of Peter's will. If his will was not changed, would it be possible to make the changes after the date of his death?

[6 marks]

c) Jenny is considering selling the estate agency business for its current value of £160,000. What would the inheritance tax implications be if this sale took place before Peter were to die, and would she be best advised to postpone the disposal until after his death when the business is likely to be worth £15,000–£20,000 less than its present value.

[5 marks]

d) Discuss how the inheritance tax liabilities might be reduced if the executors were to sell certain assets after Peter's death.

[6 marks]
[Total 25 marks]

10

3 You have been asked to provide advice at today's date (which you should assume is 6 April 1994) to Andrew Hope. Andrew is due to commence self-employment running a catering business on 1 July 1994. Andrew's wife Hilda will also be involved on a full-time basis in running the business. Both Andrew and Hilda are 45 years old, and they plan to transfer the business to their son in about 10 years time. Projected profits (before charging depreciation and any possible wages to Hilda) are as follows:

	£
Period ended 30.4.95	33,000
Year ended 30.4.96	48,000
Year ended 30.4.97	36,000

No adjustments to these figures for tax purposes are anticipated.

Andrew will acquire second-hand equipment costing £25,000 on 1 July 1994, and new equipment costing £15,000 on 1 June 1995. Second-hand equipment with an original cost of £14,000 is expected to be sold for £16,000 on 1 July 1995, and further new equipment with an expected useful life of four years and an expected nil scrap value will be acquired for £8,000 on 1 January 1996.

Andrew also has the following sources of income:

i) £125,000 in a building society account producing interest of £7,500 p.a. net of tax.

ii) An unfurnished property worth £90,000 which produces an income, net of expenses, of £9,000 p.a. Andrew is considering selling this property within the next five years, and the sale would give rise to a substantial capital gain.

Hilda currently has no income or assets in her own right.

Required:

a) Calculate Andrew's projected schedule D case 1 profits and capital allowances for 1994–95 to 1997–98 inclusive, assuming that he wishes to minimise his assessable profits.

[9 marks]

b) Outline the tax implications of Andrew employing Hilda until 30 April 1995, and then bringing her into partnership as an equal partner from 1 May 1995 onwards.

[10 marks]

c) Assuming that the strategy in (b) is followed, discuss other tax planning measures that Andrew and Hilda could take in order to minimise their overall tax liability. Your discussion should include a consideration of income tax, CGT and IHT. You should assume that future schedule D case 1 profits, net of capital allowances, will not exceed £45,000 p.a.

[6 marks]
[Total 25 marks]

4 a) Magee plc, a UK resident company with annual profits of £5,000,000, is planning to form a new 100% subsidiary, Gavin Ltd, that will carry out trading activities through a permanent establishment in Ruritania. There is no double taxation treaty between the UK and Ruritania. Magee plc does not want the company to be regarded as resident in the UK, and is considering three possible structures for Gavin Ltd, as follows:

i) Incorporation in the UK, with directors' meetings being held in Ruritania.

ii) Incorporation in Ruritania, with directors' meetings being held in the UK.

iii) Incorporation in Ruritania, with directors' meetings being held in Ruritania.

Required:
Advise Magee plc as to which of the above structures will meet its residence requirements for Gavin Ltd. Your should give reasons for your conclusions in each case.

[4 marks]

b) The main reason why Magee plc does not want Gavin Ltd to be regarded as resident in the UK, is because of the low corporation tax rate of 8% that is applicable to companies resident in Ruritania. The forecast results for Gavin Ltd's first year of trading to 31 March 1995 are as follows:

	£
Profits per accounts (before taxation)	400,000
Tax-adjusted profits:	
under Ruritanian legislation	450,000
under UK legislation	420,000

There is no withholding tax imposed on dividends paid out of Ruritania.

Required:
Assuming that Gavin Ltd is regarded as resident in Ruritania, and is classed as a controlled foreign company:

i) Explain what a controlled foreign company is. You *are not* expected to explain the various exclusion tests.

ii) Explain why it would be beneficial for Magee plc, if Gavin Ltd were to pay a dividend equivalent to at least 50% of its distributable profits. Your answer should be supported by appropriate calculations.

[9 marks]

c) Magee plc is to send Alex Tower, one of its senior executives, to Ruritania in order to carry out strategic planning duties for Gavin Ltd. Alex will continue to be employed and paid by Magee plc. He will leave the UK on 1 December 1994, and will stay in Ruritania for either 14 or 18 months depending on circumstances. During that period he will return to the UK for holidays at least once every three months, for about two weeks at a time. Alex will not suffer any taxation in Ruritania.

Required:
Explain Alex's potential liability to UK taxation while he is working in Ruritania.

[8 marks]

d) Magee plc is to send another senior employee, Tony Smith, to work in Ruritania for a period of nine months. During this period, his wife and two children, aged 15 and 20, plan to visit him twice. Tony will initially pay for all of these travelling expenses himself, both for himself and his family, but will then be reimbursed by Magee plc.

Required:
State whether these reimbursements will be taxable emoluments under Schedule E, and whether he will be able to deduct the travelling expenses under Schedule E.

[4 marks]
[Total 25 marks]

5 Holdings Ltd is an investment company which is a close company but not a close investment company. Holdings Ltd owned the following shareholdings in trading companies throughout the year ended 31 March 1995:

Grunt Ltd – 80% (acquired 1.4.86)
Shove Ltd – 100% (acquired 1.10.89)
Pink Ltd – 100% (acquired 1.4.94)

10

Grunt Ltd owns 75% of the share capital of Rose Ltd, which it acquired at par for £750 on 1 July 1986.

All the trading companies make up their accounts to 31 March. Adjusted trading profits/(losses) for the year ended 31 March 1995 were as follows:

	Grunt	*Shove*	*Pink*	*Rose*
	£	*£*	*£*	*£*
Adjusted profit/(loss)	800	62,000	85,000	(1,400)

As at 1 April 1994, Rose Ltd had unused trading losses of £2,000 and surplus ACT of £500, while Shove Ltd had unused capital losses of £8,000.

For the year ended 31 March 1995 Holdings Ltd had no income and incurred allowable management expenses of £22,000.

On 1 July 1994 Rose Ltd paid a dividend of £1,200.

On 6 May 1994 Pink Ltd sold an office building to Rose Ltd which had cost it £20,000 in June 1986. The sale to Rose Ltd was at the current market value of £170,000.

Required:

a) Briefly explain the consequences of Holdings Ltd being classed as a close company.

[5 marks]

b) Calculate the corporation tax liability for each of the companies in the Holdings group for the year ended 31 March 1995. Your answer should include an explanation of your treatment of the group's ACT and losses. You should assume that all favourable elections and claims have been, or will be, made.

[11 marks]

c) Comment on the various tax consequences which would arise if:

   i) Grunt Ltd were to sell its shares in Rose Ltd on 30 June 1995 for a substantial sum, and

   ii) Holdings Ltd were to acquire a small (under 1%) holding of shares in an overseas company, from which it would receive dividends of approximately £2,500 p.a. net of withholding tax.

   Your answer should include any relevant tax planning measures that the Holdings group could take.

   Assume the following RPIs,

June 1986	97.8
May 1994	142.9
June 1995	145.0

[9 marks]

[Total 25 marks]

6 Abdul Khan is the majority shareholder and managing director of AKF Ltd, an unquoted company running a number of retail furniture shops. He has asked for your advice on the following:

a) AKF Ltd's VAT returns are prepared on a quarterly basis. The return for the quarter to 31 January has been submitted two weeks late for the past two years due to the delay caused by the company's January sale. The same delay is expected to occur this year. Abdul wants to know the implications of this, and whether they can be avoided. The payment to HM Customs & Excise for the quarter to 31 January 1995 is expected to be £11,000. AKF Ltd makes up its accounts to 31 March, and does not qualify as a small business for VAT purposes.

b) On 1 June 1995 the company is to complete the purchase of a new shop costing £425,000, which it has had specially built and fitted out. The purchase price will include the following:

	£
Land	110,000
General electrical wiring	9,200
Central heating and related plumbing	21,800
Ventilation system	15,100
Fire alarm and sprinkler system	13,100
Additional work to comply with the fire regulations	5,800
False ceiling to hide pipes and wiring	39,500
General lighting	18,800
Lighting for displays and shop front	4,300
Shop counters	12,900
Floor tiling	11,200
Two general offices	46,500
Architects and legal fees	16,800

All figures are net of VAT, and the shop is not in an enterprise zone. Abdul wants to know which of the above items will qualify for capital allowances. He also wants an explanation as to why the various items have either qualified or not qualified for capital allowances.

c) AKF Ltd is to partly finance the purchase of its new shop by selling two old shops on 10 November 1994 for £150,000 and £175,000 respectively. The first shop cost £62,000 in November 1986, and was extended at a cost of £25,000 during December 1990. 15% of the floor space of this shop has always been let to a tenant. The second shop cost £85,000 in March 1989. The purchase price of this shop included some spare land which was sold for £30,000 in May 1989, at which time the market value of the shop and remaining land was £60,000. A capital gain of £28,000 arose on the disposal of another shop in October 1989 for £55,000. The policy of AKF Ltd is to rollover capital gains wherever possible. Advise Abdul as to the tax implications arising from the sale of these two shops.

Assume the following RPIs:

Nov 1986	99.3
Mar 1989	112.3
May 1989	115.0
Dec 1990	129.9
November 1994	144.0

d) The remaining £100,000 of the purchase price of the new shop is to be financed by either a ten year bank loan, secured on the shop, at an interest rate of 4% above the bank's base rate, or the issue of new ordinary share capital to minority shareholders. AKF Ltd has always paid a high level of dividends, and consequently has accumulated a substantial amount of surplus ACT. Abdul needs advice as to the tax implications of the two alternative financing arrangements and on any other non-tax points that are relevant.

e) AKF Ltd is to set up a scheme whereby some of the remuneration of its employees is linked to the profitability of the company. Abdul has read that such a scheme will reduce the employees' tax liability, provided that it is approved by the Inland Revenue. Abdul wants to know:

i) how such a scheme would work
ii) if he could exclude certain employees from the scheme
iii) whether he could benefit under the scheme himself, and

iv) an outline of the conditions that would have to be met in order to obtain Inland Revenue approval.

Required:
Draft a reply to each of Abdul's queries, each of which carries equal marks.

[Total 25 marks]

Answers to Section 10 begin on page 122.

MOCK EXAMINATION

In Section 9 you were given the chance to prepare for the examination by attempting a variety of examination style questions which provided a representative coverage of the whole syllabus. This Section builds on that preparation by providing a complete 'mock' exam paper typical in length and style to the one you will be sitting 'for real'. It also includes information on how marks are allocated. But remember, it is not intended as an indicator of likely topics.

To gain the most benefit from this mock exam, you should attempt it under examination conditions. When you have finished, turn to Section 14 which contains advice on how you should have approached each question.

Time allowed – 3 hours

Number of questions on paper – 6

FOUR questions ONLY should be attempted

Rates of tax and allowances are on pages 3–5

1 Abigail is the sole owner of a fashion retail business. She will transfer the business as a going concern to a limited company, Abigail Ltd, on 30 November 1994.

Abigail has always made up her accounts to 31 May and her recent profits as adjusted for tax purposes have been agreed as follows:

	£
Year ended 31 May 1990	35,000
Year ended 31 May 1991	41,000
Year ended 31 May 1992	45,000
Year ended 31 May 1993	48,000
Year ended 31 May 1994	51,000
Period to 30 November 1994	28,000

Abigail owned assets which had written down values as at 6 April 1991 as follows:

	£
Plant and equipment	16,000
Motor car	7,800

On 1 August 1991 she purchased some new display cabinets at a cost of £8,600 and on 1 November 1993 she purchased a new motor car at a cost of £15,000. The old car was disposed of on the same date for £2,000.

The Inspector of Taxes has agreed that Abigail uses both motor cars 60% for business purposes.

The market values of the assets at the time of their transfer to the company were:

	£
Goodwill	50,000
Freehold premises	95,000
Plant and equipment	18,000
Motor car	11,000
Net current assets	31,000

The goodwill has no acquisition cost.

The freehold premises were acquired on 1 July 1984 at a cost of £45,000.

All of the items of plant and equipment are moveable and no item cost more than £6,000.

Abigail Ltd will have 10,000 ordinary shares of £1 each. Abigail will own 97% of the shares. Her father will subscribe for the remaining 3%.

Abigail has not yet finalised how the consideration for the transfer of the business is to be settled. She has no available funds to meet any taxation liabilities arising as a result of the transfer. She would therefore like to obtain some of the consideration in cash while, at the same time, minimising any taxation liabilities.

Required:

a) Calculate Abigail's net schedule DI assessments for the final four years of trading, assuming that all beneficial elections are made.

[11 marks]

b) Calculate the chargeable gains arising on the transfer of the business and advise Abigail how her liability to CGT can be minimised.

[6 marks]

c) Explain the VAT consequences arising as a result of the transfer of the business.

[4 marks]

d) If the business should fail, advise Abigail's father how he may claim relief for his capital loss on the shares subscribed for.

[4 marks]

Assume the following RPIs:

July 1984	89.1
November 1994	144.2

[Total 25 marks]

2 Richard and Judy Finlay, aged 42 and 45 years respectively, are the principal shareholders and directors of Morning Ltd, an unquoted trading company. The share capital of Morning Ltd consists of 100,000 £1 ordinary shares, of which Richard owns 40,000 and Judy 20,000. Their son Anthony has recently been made a director of Morning Ltd, and the couple has decided to make him a gift of 20,000 of their shares on 1 December 1994. The value of Morning Ltd's shares agreed by the Inland Revenue is as follows:

Shareholding	*Value per share*
	£
20%	8
40%	12
60%	17
80%	23

Richard originally acquired 24,000 shares at par on 1 July 1977, the date of Morning Ltd's incorporation, and purchased a further 8,000 shares on 1 August 1986 for £30,000. On 1 May 1990 Morning Ltd had a 1 for 4 rights issue at the market value at that date of £5 per share which Richard took up in full. The market value of Morning Ltd's shares at 31 March 1982 was £2 per share. Judy's shares had originally been acquired by her mother upon Morning Ltd's incorporation. She inherited them when her mother died on 30 September 1989, the shares being included in her estate at a value of £90,000. Judy did not take up her entitlement in the rights issue, but sold her rights to another director for £1,200.

Neither Richard nor Judy have made any previous transfers of value for inheritance tax purposes.

Required:

a) Calculate the chargeable gain arising assuming that the gift of 20,000 Morning Ltd shares to Anthony is made by (i) Richard and (ii) Judy.

[15 marks]

b) Calculate the value of the gift for inheritance tax purposes assuming it is made by (i) Richard and (ii) Judy, and explain whether it will be chargeable to IHT.

[10 marks]

You should assume that the 1994/95 inheritance tax rates and reliefs apply in the future. Also assume the following RPIs:

March 1982	79.4
August 1986	97.8
September 1989	116.6
May 1990	126.2
December 1994	144.0

[Total 25 marks]

3 Minders Ltd is a close company that buys and sells second hand cars. The company is controlled by Arthur and Terry, who each own half of its ordinary share capital. Arthur is the managing director of the company, Terry is neither a director nor an employee.

Minders Ltd was incorporated on 1 November 1993. On 1 March 1994 the company acquired business premises which were in a bad state of repair, and it immediately started to repair and refurbish them. On 1 April 1994 expenditure was incurred on an advertising campaign. The company commenced purchasing cars for resale on 1 June 1994, but the business premises were not opened until 1 July 1994. On the same day the company registered for VAT and made its first sale. Accounts have been prepared for the period 1 November 1993 to 31 March 1995.

On 1 September 1994, Minders Ltd bought a new 1,300 cc motor car costing £11,000 (including VAT), for the use of Arthur, and a new 1,600 cc motor car costing £14,000 (including VAT) for the use of Terry. During 1994–95 Arthur drove 1,600 miles on company business, Terry had no business mileage. No private fuel is provided by the company.

On 1 December 1994, Minders Ltd made an interest free loan of £31,000 to Terry, which he used to purchase a yacht. The loan has not yet been repaid.

Required:

a) i) Identify Minders Ltd's accounting periods up to and including, 31 March 1995.

ii) How will Minders Ltd's expenditure on its advertising campaign and the refurbishment of its business premises be treated for the purposes of corporation tax and VAT?

[9 marks]

b) Explain how Minders Ltd should account for VAT on the purchase and sale of its second-hand cars.

[4 marks]

c) Explain the tax implications, for both Minders Ltd and Arthur and Terry, arising from the provision of the new company motor cars.

[8 marks]

d) Advise both Minders Ltd and Terry of the tax implications arising from the provision of the interest free loan.

[4 marks]
[Total 25 marks]

4 Priam was born in the country of Wantai, but has lived and worked in the UK for many years. He has the following assets and liabilities, all of which are shown in sterling:

a) His main residence consisting of freehold property situated in the UK worth £95,000.

b) A residence in Wantai worth £45,000.

c) 20,000 shares in Wantan Inc., a company quoted on the Wantai stock exchange at 300 – 316 with recorded bargains of 300, 304 and 314.

d) Antiques worth £30,000 which are situated in his Wantai residence.

e) A loan of £16,000 due to Priam by his brother who is resident in Wantai. The brother used the loan to buy a cottage situated in the UK.

f) Jewellery worth £25,000 that was bought in Wantai, but is now situated in the UK.

g) Bank deposits in sterling of £28,000 with the UK Branch of the Wantai National Bank.

h) UK government stocks with a nominal value of £15,000, quoted at 98 – 102.

j) Wantai government stocks valued at £19,000.

k) Gambling debts of £1,200 are due by Priam to a debtor resident in the UK.

All of Priam's estate is left to his sister under his will.

Required:

a) Explain the rules determining whether Priam is domiciled in the UK for the purpose of IHT.

[6 marks]

b) State, giving reasons, which of the above assets are situated in the UK for the purposes of IHT.

[5 marks]

c) i) Calculate Priam's liability to IHT if he were to die in the near future and be treated as NOT domiciled in the UK.

ii) Calculate by what amount Priam's liability to IHT in (i) would increase if he were instead treated as domiciled in the UK.

You should use the IHT rates for 1994/95, and assume that Wantai death duty of £50,000 would be payable on Priam's death in respect of his assets situated in that country. There is no double taxation treaty between the UK and Wantai.

[14 marks]
[Total 25 marks]

5 You are the tax adviser to Blackwells plc, the holding company for a group of companies involved in the brewing industry. Blackwells plc has recently completed the purchase of Brownleys Ltd, buying 100% of its share capital. This company was purchased because of the large number of public houses that it owns in desirable locations. However, Brownleys Ltd has been badly managed, and currently has substantial unutilised trading losses and a small amount of surplus ACT.

Over a five-year period Blackwells plc plans to wind down the trade of Brownleys Ltd as follows:

a) Those premises that are in desirable locations will be transferred to various other group companies, and used by them.

b) Those premises that are no longer required will be sold by Brownleys Ltd, with the proceeds being used to finance the purchase of new premises by other group companies. These new premises will consist of both freehold properties and leasehold properties. The sale of Brownleys Ltd's premises will result in substantial capital gains.

Blackwells plc recently adopted the same policy with another purchased company, Whiteleys Ltd, although the premises sold in that instance mostly resulted in capital losses.

The other companies in the group are variously owned between 51% and 100% by Blackwells plc.

Required:
Draft a report to Blackwells plc covering the tax implications arising from:

a) Its proposed treatment of Brownleys Ltd.

b) Its proposed treatment of Brownleys Ltd's premises.

c) The proposed purchase of new freehold and leasehold premises by other group companies.

You should include tax planning advice as appropriate.

[Total 25 marks]

6 Jason Orange is single and has been a self-employed dancer for the past five years. His tax-adjusted profits have consistently been £30,000 p.a. Jason has recently been offered the leading role in a London musical. The contract will be for an initial period of one year, but may be renewed if the show is successful. The contract would commence on 1 August 1994. The first month would be spent in rehearsals. From 1 September 1994, Jason would be required to perform eight shows a week: evenings from Monday to Saturday inclusive, and matinees on Wednesday and Saturday. His contract would also require him to take part in any publicity required by the show's producers, and would prevent him from undertaking work for anyone else. Jason would be permitted a break of one month in February, during which his understudy would perform his role.

Jason has been offered a fee of £35,000 for this year-long contract. He is concerned that if the Inland Revenue decide to class him as an employee, this may lead to a drop in his post-tax income.

Jason is also anxious to make provision for his future. He realises that opportunities for dancing will decrease as he gets older and he is also concerned that injury may curtail his career. A friend has suggested that he should provide for a pension. Jason considers this to be sensible advice but is reluctant to tie up his capital for such a long period of time. He has heard about personal equity plans and life assurance policies and wonders whether these would be more suitable for his needs. Jason is currently 28 and as yet has made no pension provisions.

Required:

a) Outline the criteria which would be used to determine whether Jason will be classified as employed or self-employed.

[7 marks]

b) Assuming that Jason accepts the contract to perform in the London musical, and is classified by the Inland Revenue as employed, advise him of whether or not this will result in a reduction in his post-tax income compared to his present earnings from self-employment. Your answer should be supported by appropriate calculations.

[6 marks]

c) Explain the differing tax implications of investing in:

i) a personal pension scheme
ii) a personal equity plan and
iii) a life assurance policy.

Your answer should identify the maximum amount which Jason could invest under each option. You should also comment on the liquidity and risk of each of these investments.

[12 marks]

[Total 25 marks]

Answers to Section 11 begin on page 132.

ANSWERS TO EXAM STYLE QUESTIONS

Once you have attempted the questions in Section 9, you should read the advice given below on what the examiner will be looking for in a good answer. The indicative content for each answer is given in detail.

1 a) i) The legal fees of £600 re a dispute over the boundary of a field are allowable as they are incurred in the protection of an asset. No adjustment was necessary in calculating Owen's adjusted loss.

ii) The amortisation of £800 needed to be added back in calculating Owen's adjusted loss. An allowance would then be given in each of the ten years of the lease:

	£
Premium	8,000
Less: £8,000 × 2% × (10 – 1)	(1,440)
Assessable on landlord	6,560

Allowable to Owen: £6,560/10 years = £656 p.a.

iii) The compensation of £900 for damaged crops is of a revenue nature and is therefore assessable. No adjustment was therefore necessary in calculating Owen's loss.

iv) The lease payments are in respect of an expensive car (costing over £12,000) and a proportion must therefore have been added back:

	£
Lease payments	3,000
$£3{,}000 \times \dfrac{£12{,}000 + 1/2\,(16{,}000 - 12{,}000)}{16{,}000}$	(2,625)
Disallow	375

v) The annual subscription of £48 to the *Pig Breeders' Gazette* would appear to be wholly and exclusively for the purposes of Owen's trade. No adjustment was therefore necessary in calculating his adjusted loss.

b) *Owen MacDonald's tax position*

	1994/95	*1995/96*
	£	£
Schedule D (averaged – 15,000/2)	7,500	7,500
Capital allowances:		
P & M £10,000 × 25%	(2,500)	
(10,000 – 2,500) × 25%		(1,875)
ABA £12,000 × 4%	(480)	(480)
	4,520	5,145
Loss claim s.380 ICTA 1988	(4,520)	–
	–	5,145
Personal allowance	–	(3,445)
Taxable income	–	1,700

Relief for the married couple's allowance is given by means of a tax credit.

Capital gain	12,000
Loss claim s.72 FA 1991: (8,500 – 4,520) =	(3,980)
	8,020
Annual exemption	(5,800)
Chargeable gain	2,220

Averaging of farmers profits has been claimed so as to transfer income to 1995/96 and therefore utilise Owen's personal allowance for that year. The unused balance of the married couple's allowance can be transferred to Olive. This treatment of Owen's loss wastes his personal allowance for 1994/95, but this is unavoidable as loss relief against capital gains under section 72 FA 1991 cannot be claimed unless a claim against income under section 380 ICTA 1988 has already been made.

Claims will have to be made as follows:

- ▶ By 5 April 1997 in respect of loss relief
- ▶ By 5 April 1998 for the averaging of profits
- ▶ By 5 April 2001 and 2002 to transfer the unused married couple's allowance for each year respectively.

c) The advice given to Cindy is very misleading for a number of reasons:

i) Cindy Ltd would be a close investment company and, as such, would be liable to pay corporation tax at the standard rate of 33% irrespective of the level of profits.

ii) Directors' remuneration is deductible as a management expense, but the figure charged would need to be justifiable. The Revenue would probably only allow a small percentage of the income – perhaps 10%.

iii) Any directors' fees voted would incur employers' NIC at 10.2% plus employees' class 1 NIC unless Cindy already pays the maximum class 1 contributions.

iv) The deduction of Cindy's salary and the employers' NIC contributions would result in a loss each year. As this loss belongs to Cindy Ltd, which would have no other income, it could only be carried forward.

v) Dividends received by a company are franked investment income and are not liable to corporation tax. The company could claim a repayment of the ACT suffered, but only to the extent that its management expenses are allowed.

vi) Cindy could not provide for a pension out of her director's remuneration as such earnings from an investment company do not count as net relevant earnings.

vii) A future disposal of the shares by Cindy Ltd would generate a capital gain chargeable at 33%. If Cindy wished to liquidate the company in order to extract the disposal proceeds, she would incur a further CGT liability as she would be deemed to be disposing of the shares in Cindy Ltd. This double CGT charge could be avoided by Cindy Ltd paying a dividend to Cindy prior to liquidation, but this still involves an element of double taxation as Cindy Ltd would have to account for ACT and the dividend would be chargeable to income tax in Cindy's hands.

2 a) The first consideration is whether the expenditure is capital or revenue. The dividing line between capital and revenue expenditure is not clear. In *O'Grady* v *Bullcroft Main Collieries* the cost of rebuilding a factory chimney was held to be capital. Whereas similar expenditure in the case of *Samuel Jones & Co* v *CIR* was allowed as revenue on the grounds that the chimney was an integral part of the building.

Rudyard plc's expenditure will probably be regarded as capital as the entire wall is being replaced rather than merely repaired. The amount of expenditure involved would also support the view that this is capital (*Phillips* v *Whieldon Sanitary Potteries*).

The second consideration is whether the wall is a separate asset or part of the factory. If the wall is considered to be a separate asset, there will be no tax relief for this capital expenditure. If the wall is regarded as part of the factory, the expenditure will qualify for industrial buildings allowance (IBA) of 4% per annum, commencing in the accounts year in which the expenditure is incurred.

Rudyard plc's wall surrounds the factory premises. This implies that the wall is a separate asset rather than being an integral part of the factory. Thus it is likely that no capital allowances will be available.

The provision for repairs in the accounts for the year ended 31 March 1994 will need to be disallowed in computing the company's Schedule DI profits, as expenditure can only be allowed when incurred.

(**Note:** marks will be awarded for knowledge and general reasoning and not for the conclusions actually reached).

b) The cost of land (including the legal fees) never qualifies for tax relief. If the site is rented, however, the rental costs are deductible as they are revenue expenditure.

The government grant is deducted in computing the cost of the building eligible for IBA. The balance of £520,000 may qualify for IBA, provided that the showrooms and shops account for less than 25% of the expenditure. The expenditure devoted to the shops should therefore be reduced by at least 5% and reallocated to the warehouse. Failure to make these changes will result in the reduction of the eligible cost to £364,000 (£520,000 × 70%).

Assuming that the changes to the expenditure are made, a writing down allowance of £20,800 (£520,000 × 4%) will be given annually, commencing in the accounts year in which the building is brought into industrial use (i.e. 31 March 1996).

c) The cost of acquiring the premises is capital and thus not deductible in computing schedule DI profits. This cost will not qualify for IBA unless the premises are situated in an enterprise zone. The roof repairs will not be deductible as they are pre-ownership delapidations (*Law Shipping Co* v *CIR*).

The conversion costs will need to be apportioned in determining how much qualifies for capital allowances. The Finance Act 1994 sets out a table of expenditure which is regarded as part of a building and thus ineligible for capital allowance as plant and machinery. The fixtures and fittings, and the costs of securing them, will probably qualify as plant and machinery. The partitions will probably not qualify as these appear to have become part of the building (this can be distinguished from the situation in *Jarrold* v *John Good and Sons*). The suspended ceilings and the floor and wall tiles will also not qualify. They will be regarded as part of the building following the decision in *Wimpy International* v *Warland*. The special lighting will qualify if Rudyard plc can show that it fulfils a specific function. The company could perhaps argue that bright lighting is essential in a supermarket.

Expenditure qualifying for capital allowances will be added to the general pool during the accounts year ended 31 March 1995. A writing down allowance of 25% will be given.

d) Assuming that option (i) is chosen, the CGT implications are as follows:

	Cost	*March 1982*
	£	£
Disposal proceeds	120,000	120,000
Cost/March 1982 value	(25,000)	(70,000)
Enhancement expenditure	(12,000)	(12,000)
Unindexed gain	83,000	38,000
Indexation: £70,000 × 0.800 (restricted)	(56,000)	(38,000)
£12,000 × 0.132 (restricted)	(1,584)	(–)
Gain/(loss)	25,416	–

Indexation can no longer create or increase an allowable loss. Thus the disposal will give rise to neither a gain nor a loss.

If option (ii) is chosen, it will be necessary to value the contingent right to receive the additional consideration (*Marren* v *Ingles*). This value must be added to the disposal proceeds of £100,000 in calculating the chargeable gain arising on the disposal of the shop. Once the position regarding the planning permission has been finalised, a further CGT computation will be made. Any additional cash received will be chargeable to the extent that it exceeds the value of the right plus any indexation due. If no additional consideration is received, the right will become valueless and an allowable loss will result.

3 a) If the partners decide to claim relief under s380, the loss will be allocated according to the profit sharing ratio for the 1993/94 fiscal year:

	Total	*Mary*	*Mungo*	*Midge*
	£	£	£	£
Salary	7,500	–	–	7,500
Balance	(25,500)	(14,025)	(5,100)	(6,375)
Loss to 31/12/93	(18,000)	(14,025)	(5,100)	1,125
Reallocation		825	300	(1,125)
	(18,000)	(13,200)	(4,800)	–
Loss from 1/1/94	(6,000)	(3,900)	(1,500)	(600)
	(24,000)	(17,100)	(6,300)	(600)

The notional profit has been reallocated between the partners as follows:

Mary £1,125 × 14,025/19,125 = 825

Mungo £1,125 × 5,100/19,125 = 300

A claim under s380, to set the loss off against 1993/94 statutory total income must be made by 5 April 1996. A claim may also be made against 1994/95 statutory total income if, for example, any partner is in receipt of income from outside the partnership. Such a claim must be made by 5 April 1997. Claims under s380 frequently result in the loss of personal allowances.

Once a claim under s380 has been made, it is possible to set any balance of loss against capital gains of the same year.

If the partners decide to claim relief under s385, the loss will be allocated according to the profit sharing ratio for the accounts year ended 31 October 1993:

	Total	*Mary*	*Mungo*	*Midge*
	£	£	£	£
Salary	10,000	–	–	10,000
Balance	(34,000)	(18,700)	(6,800)	(8,500)
	(24,000)	(18,700)	(6,800)	1,500
Reallocation		1,100	400	(1,500)
	(24,000)	(17,600)	(6,400)	–

The notional profit has been reallocated as follows:

Mary £1,500 × 18,700/25,500 = £1,100
Mungo £1,500 × 6,800/25,500 = £400

Losses claimed under s385 are set against future schedule DI profits of the same trade. A claim to establish the amount of the loss must be made within six years of the end of the year of the loss.

Each partner may make his or her own decision in respect of the loss.

b) Prior to claiming relief for the loss, Mary's 1993/94 income tax and national insurance liabilities were as follows:

	£
Income	20,000
50% class 4 NIC	(493)
Personal allowance	(3,445)
Taxable income	16,062
Tax due:	
£3,000 × 20%	600
£13,062 × 25%	3,265
	3,865
NIC due:	
(20,000 – 6,490) × 7.3%	986
	4,851

Claiming relief for the loss of £17,100 available under s380 will reduce Mary's profits to £2,900. As this is below her personal allowance, and below the lower limit for class 4 NIC, she will receive a repayment of the full £4,851 computed above.

In addition, Mary would still have £500 of loss available to carry forward under s385 (£17,600 – £17,100). As she is liable to higher rate tax in 1995/96, this will result in a saving of £200 (500 × 40%).

If Mary claims her full loss of £17,600 in 1995/96 under s385, she will save tax of £7,040 (17,600 × 40%). No NIC saving will result as her profits will still exceed the upper limit of £22,360.

So notwithstanding the delay in obtaining relief, Mary should be advised to claim relief under s385 as its results in an additional saving of £1,989 (7,040 – 4,851 – 200).

c) Any capital gains arising on the disposal of government securities are exempt from capital gains tax. Although Mary has not received any interest from her government securities, she will still be chargeable to income tax in respect of the accrued income included within her sale proceeds. The accrued income scheme only applies if the securities held have a nominal value in excess of £5,000. This accrued income is chargeable under schedule DVI. The amount chargeable is £10,000 × 12% × 5/12 = £500.

Note: accrued income is actually calculated on a daily basis, but for examination purposes it is acceptable for the calculation to be made on a monthly basis.

d) i) Where services are supplied over a period of time, the tax point is the earliest of three dates:

- ▶ the date on which the service is completed
- ▶ the date a tax invoice is issued
- ▶ the date payment is received.

If an invoice is issued within 14 days of the service being completed, the date of the invoice will be substituted for the date the service is completed.

ii) The partnership's return for the quarter ended 31 July 1994 must include the output tax due in respect of the payment received on 1 June 1994. The return will not include the output tax due in respect of the balance of the purchase price because (as the invoice was issued within 14 days of the work being completed) the invoice date falls into the following quarter.

Input tax cannot be recovered in respect of the materials used personally by Mungo.

The return will therefore show the following VAT due:

	£
Outputs: £5,000 × 7/47 =	744.68
Inputs: (3,000 – 500) × 17.5% =	(437.50)
VAT due by 30 August 1994	307.18

iii) The input tax suffered on entertaining expenditure is not deductible, so the partnership overclaimed £25.32 (£170 × 7/47). This, together with the understated output tax of £300, gives a total understatement of £325.32. As the total error is less than £2,000, it can be corrected by inclusion in the return for the current quarter. Correction in this way will mean that no penalties are incurred.

iv) The cash accounting scheme would allow the partnership to account for VAT on the basis of cash received and cash paid. As the partnership pays in cash for all purchases, this will make no difference to the dates on which input tax can be reclaimed. If the business gives credit, however, it will delay the payment of output tax on any supplies made. In addition, the scheme gives automatic relief for bad debts.

4 a) **Income tax implications**

As the business is changing from a sole tradership to a partnership the trade is deemed to cease. The Schedule D Case I cessation rules will operate:

		£
1992/93	PYB y/e 30/6/91	49,764
1993/94	PYB y/e 30/6/92	58,176
1994/95	Actual £62,520 × 3/12	15,630

The Revenue will invoke s63 and amend the 1992/93 and 1993/94 assessments to actual, as this results in increased assessments:

		£
1992/93	(58,176 × 3/12) + (65,304 × 9/12)	63,522
1993/94	(65,304 × 3/12) + (62,520 × 9/12)	63,216

As the new partnership is commencing after 6 April 1994 it will be subject to the new current year basis of assessment:

		£
1994/95	Actual £66,096 × 9/12	49,572
1995/96	CYB y/e 30/6/95	66,096

The assessments, assuming that the business is treated as ceasing, will therefore total £258,036.

Note that the profits of £49,572 arising between 1 July 1994 and 5 April 1995 have been assessed twice. They will therefore be eligible for overlap relief. This is given either when the business ceases, or for any earlier year of assessment for which the basis period exceeds twelve months.

The partners have the option of making a continuation election under s113(2) ICTA 1988. Making this election will avoid the operation of the new current year basis of assessment. The preceding year basis of assessment will instead continue to be applied:

		£
1992/93	PYB y/e 30/6/91	49,764
1993/94	PYB y/e 30/6/92	58,176
1994/95	PYB y/e 30/6/93	65,304
1995/96	PYB y/e 30/6/94	62,520
		235,764

Notwithstanding the overlap relief mentioned above, which may not be given for many years, the partners should probably be advised to make the continuation election as it results in reduced assessments.

The election must be made in writing and signed by both partners within two years of the date of Brian's admission to the partnership.

Whichever option is chosen, Brian will pay tax on his share of the 1994/95 Schedule D assessment.

VAT implications

The partnership is regarded as a separate entity from the sole tradership and will therefore need to register for VAT. Mr Yates should deregister as a sole trader. However, it is possible for the partnership to take over Mr Yates' existing VAT registration number. This will involve assuming all Mr Yates' existing VAT liabilities.

No VAT arises on the transfer of the business assets as the business is being transferred as a going concern.

b) **Implications for Brian**

As an employee, Brian would have been liable to the maximum class 1 contributions as his salary exceeded the upper limit of £22,360 (52 weeks x £430). These will have been collected through the PAYE system. As he was a member of an occupational pension scheme, he may have been contracted out of the state earnings related pension scheme (SERPS), in which case he would have been paying his contributions at the reduced contracted out rate. Earnings for the purpose of class 1 contributions are before the deduction of pension contributions or capital allowances.

As a partner, Brian will be liable to class 2 contributions at the rate of £5.65 per week. These will either be collected by direct debit or paid quarterly in arrears. In addition, Brian will be liable to class 4 contributions, for which the maximum is

£1,158.51 ((£22,360 – £6,490) × 7.3%). These will be collected by the Inland Revenue along with the income tax due under Schedule DI (i.e. 50% on 1 January in the year of assessment and 50% on the following 1 July). Half of the class 4 contributions will be deductible in computing Brian's statutory total income. Earnings for the purpose of class 4 contributions are after the deduction of capital allowances (but not pension contributions).

Implications for Mr Yates

As an employer, Mr Yates would have been responsible for paying employers' class 1 NIC. There is no upper earnings limit, therefore the contributions would have been based on Brian's full salary of £25,000. These contributions would have been paid under the PAYE system and were deductible in computing Mr Yates' Schedule DI profits.

Once Brian has joined the partnership, each partner is responsible for his own NIC.

c) Under the Enterprise Investment Scheme, income tax relief is available in respect of new equity investment in unquoted trading companies. Mr Yates may invest a minimum of £500 and a maximum of £100,000 per fiscal year. Income tax relief is restricted to the lower rate of 20% and is given by means of a tax credit.

Relief on half the amount invested between 6 April and 5 October can be carried back to the preceding tax year, subject to a maximum carry back of £15,000.

Any gain arising on the first disposal of shares acquired under the scheme will be exempt from capital gains tax, provided that relief has not been withdrawn. Relief will be withdrawn if Mr Yates disposes of the shares within five years. Relief will also be withdrawn if, within three years of the date on which the shares were issued, the company ceases to be a qualifying company, or if Mr Yates receives value from the company. Mr Yates will be treated as having received value if Gold Ltd:

- redeems or purchases his share capital
- makes a loan to him, other than an ordinary trade debt
- waives any liability of his to the company
- provides any benefits to him.

Relief is withdrawn by means of a Schedule D VI assessment for the year of assessment for which the relief was given.

EIS relief will not be available if Mr Yates is connected with Gold Ltd. He will be regarded as connected if he owns, together with associates, more than 30% of Gold Ltd's ordinary share capital, or if he is an employee or director of Gold Ltd. However, after the issue of the shares it will be possible for Mr Yates to become a paid employee or director of Gold Ltd without affecting his entitlement to EIS relief.

5 a) **Income tax consequences**

Schedule DI cessation rules

The transfer of an unincorporated business to a limited company is treated as a permanent discontinuance of the original trade. The Schedule D Case I cessation rules will, therefore, be applied to the profits earned up to the date of the transfer.

If the business was to continue in its present form the amounts assessed would be computed using the preceding year basis of assessment:

		£
1994/95	a/cs to 30/10/93	33,000
1993/94	a/cs to 30/10/92	29,000
1992/93	a/cs to 30/10/91	22,000

If the trade is treated as ceasing, the Revenue will apply s63 (because profits are rising) and assess the profits of the penultimate and antepenultimate years on an actual basis. The accounts to October 1994 will be increased by £5,000 which represents the profit arising on the sale of the stock to Barlow Limited:

		£
1994/95	(43,000 × 7/12)	25,083
1993/94	(33,000 × 7/12) + (43,000 × 5/12)	37,167
1992/93	(29,000 × 7/12) + (33,000 × 5/12)	30,667

As can be seen above, if the business ceases there will be a reduction in the profits assessed on Mr Barlow for 1994/95. Barlow Limited will, however, be liable to corporation tax on the profits earned from 1 November 1994.

Mr Barlow's liability will be increased for 1992/93 and 1993/94 owing to the operation of the cessation rules. This will result in additional income tax liability of £6,734 (increased assessments of £16,834 × 40%).

Capital allowances

	£
1991/92 (1/11/89 – 30/10/90)	
WDV b/f	8,000
WDA	(2,000)
	6,000
1992/93 (1/11/90 – 5/4/93)	
Addition	3,000
	9,000
WDA	(2,250)
	6,750
1993/94 (6/4/93 – 5/4/94)	
WDA	(1,688)
	5,062
1994/95 (6/4/94 – 30/10/94)	
Disposal at market value	(6,000)
Balancing charge	(938)

This balancing charge can be avoided by electing to transfer the assets at their written down values. In order to make this election the following conditions must be met:

- the transferor must have control over the transferee
- both parties must be liable to UK tax
- the claim must be made jointly, in writing, within two years of the transfer.

Capital gains tax consequences

The transfer of the business to a limited company is treated as a disposal for CGT purposes. As the disposal is to a connected person the assets are deemed to be transferred at their open market values.

Plant – no CGT liability arises as the items of plant are chattels each with a value of less than £6,000.

Stock and *debtors* are exempt from CGT.

12

Goodwill – the gain is the market value of £85,000. There is no March 1982 value and therefore no indexation allowance.

Premises

	Cost
	£
Disposal proceeds	100,000
Cost/March 1982 value	(75,000)
Unindexed gain	25,000
Indexation: £75,000 × 0.108	(8,100)
Gain	16,900

$$\frac{143.9 - 129.9}{129.9} = 0.108$$

The total gains on the transfer of the business will therefore be £101,900 (£85,000 + £16,900).

As the proceeds of the transfer are partly in shares, the gains will automatically be rolled over into the cost of the shares. This will postpone the payment of CGT until the shares are sold. For this relief to apply, all the business assets (with the possible exception of cash) must be transferred to the company. Here the consideration is partly in shares and partly in the form of a loan, this will result in part of the gain remaining chargeable. The amount rolled over is computed as follows:

$$\text{Total gain} \times \frac{\text{Value of shares}}{\text{Total consideration}}$$

The total consideration is as follows:

	£
Capital account	52,500
Goodwill	85,000
Revaluation of premises	25,000
Profit on stock	5,000
Total consideration	167,500

As Mr Barlow has capital losses of £11,000 brought forward and an annual exemption of £5,800 he only requires £85,100 of the gain to be rolled over. The amount of shares that should be issued is therefore £139,885 (167,500 × 85,100/101,900). This will enable £85,100 of gain to be rolled over (101,900 × 139,885/167,500). This relief is compulsory and therefore does need to be claimed.

The balance of the consideration of £27,615 (167,500 – 139,885) should remain outstanding on loan account.

VAT consequences

The transfer of a business as a going concern is not normally treated as a supply for VAT purposes provided that:

- ▶ the transferee uses the assets in the same kind of business as that carried on by the transferor
- ▶ the transferee is a taxable person or becomes so as a result of the transfer.

Barlow Limited will have to register for VAT in its own right. It can agree with Customs and Excise to take over the registration number of Mr Barlow, but this will result in the company inheriting Mr Barlow's liabilities.

b) **Extracting profits**

Mr Barlow could extract profits in the form of dividends. Such dividends are grossed up by the lower rate of tax. If Mr Barlow is a basic rate taxpayer, no further tax is due. If he becomes liable to higher rate tax, however, he will have to account to the Revenue for the additional 20% due.

Assuming that Mr Barlow will have no other sources of income, he could receive dividends of (23,700 + 3,445) × 80% = £21,716 without incurring additional liability. Although this sum falls short of the £24,000 required, he would, in addition, be entitled to an income tax refund of £689 (3,445 × 20%).

To make up his income to the £24,000 required, Mr Barlow could make withdrawals from his loan account. These would be free of tax.

From the company's point of view it would be wise to ensure that any ACT suffered could be fully recovered against any corporation tax payable. The timing of the dividend payments would also need to be considered as ACT is payable prior to any MCT liability.

6 a) Pre-trading expenditure incurred by a company within seven years of the commencement of trading is treated as an expense incurred on the first day of trading. The advertising costs (net of recoverable VAT) will therefore be deductible in computing the company's schedule DI profits. The expenditure on the car and office equipment will not be deductible under schedule DI as it is capital expenditure, but will qualify for capital allowances.

VAT on services incurred within six months of the date of registration may be recovered. So Mr Cockles can claim input tax of £446.80 (£3,000 × 7/47) in respect of the advertising. VAT can also be recovered on assets held at the date of registration. Mr Cockles can recover input tax of £1,191.48 (£8,000 × 7/47) on the office equipment. Input tax on private motor cars is not recoverable. Claims for these amounts of recoverable input tax should be made on Mr Cockle's first VAT return.

b) Whelks Ltd is required to register for VAT if there is reason to believe that its supplies will exceed the VAT registration threshold of £45,000 within the next 30 days. As Whelks Ltd's sales are projected to be £50,000 per month, it should therefore register within the first 30 days of trading. The registration will take effect from the first day of trading (i.e. 1 November 1994).

Late registration will not avoid VAT liability. Customs will simply backdate the registration and collect any output tax that should have been accounted for. This output tax is 7/47 of Whelks Ltd's sales. In addition, a penalty of 10% of the tax due will be imposed. The penalty can only be avoided if there is a reasonable excuse for the delay. Shortage of funds is specifically disallowed as a reasonable excuse. Default interest may also be charged from the date the return should have been submitted until the date of payment.

c) Commercial buildings situated in enterprise zones qualify for industrial buildings allowance. An initial allowance of 100% is available, which may be wholly or partly disclaimed. If disclaimed, a writing down allowance of 25%, calculated using the straight line method, is available instead. The cost of land never qualifies for allowances, so Whelks Ltd's claim will be limited to £100,000.

d) For Nick Salmon, any payment to induce him to join Whelks Ltd would be taxable under Schedule E irrespective of whether it is paid by Whelks Ltd or by Mr Cockles. The case of *Glantre Engineering* v *Goodhand* held that such a payment is to secure future services for the company. An emolument does not necessarily have to be paid by the employer in order to be taxable, it merely has

12 to be received by reason of the (future) employment. Nick could try to argue that the payment was compensation for losing the security of his employment with the multinational company, in which case it would not be taxable, but this argument is unlikely to be accepted.

If the payment is made by Whelks Ltd it will be deductible in computing the company's schedule DI profits as it would be regarded as the payment of emoluments. If it is made by Mr Cockles personally, no relief will be due. If Mr Cockles succeeds in arguing that the payment was gratuitous, it will be regarded as a transfer of value for inheritance tax purposes.

e) The payment of £500 per month is a round sum allowance. As it is specifically for entertaining, it should be added back in computing Whelks Ltd's schedule DI profits. Any VAT suffered is not recoverable, so the VAT inclusive cost will be disallowed. The allowance will be included in Mr Salmon's Schedule E emoluments. It should strictly be put through the PAYE scheme. Mr Salmon will be able to claim a deduction in respect of any (VAT inclusive) expenditure incurred wholly, exclusively and necessarily in the performance of his duties. He should retain receipts in order to support such a claim.

f) Whelks Ltd is a close company. Relief is available for the interest paid on a loan to acquire shares in a close company provided that the borrower either (i) owns at least 5% of the company's ordinary share capital or (ii) owns any ordinary share capital and works for the greater part of his time in the management of the company. If the borrower recovers any capital from the company, he is treated as having repaid the loan and the interest relief is reduced accordingly.

7 a) The capital gain arising on the disposal of the property is as follows:

	Cost	March 1982
	£	£
Disposal proceeds	250,000	250,000
Less expenses	(4,000)	(4,000)
	246,000	246,000
Cost/March 1982 value	(80,000)	(70,000)
Enhancement expenditure	(8,000)	(8,000)
Unindexed gain	158,000	168,000
Indexation: £80,000 × 0.811	(64,880)	(64,880)
£8,000 × 0.616	(4,928)	(4,928)
Chargeable gain	88,192	98,192

As the sisters have never used the property as their principal private residence, they will be unable to have any periods of ownership deemed to be periods of occupation. They will also be unable to benefit from letting relief.

The lower gain of £88,192 will be shared equally between Jane and Christine. Each sister will therefore be charged on £44,096.

b) In order to claim reinvestment relief, Jane must reinvest her gain in a qualifying unquoted company. A manufacturing company would seem to qualify, assuming it is carried on commercially with a view to the realisation of profits.

Jane must acquire ordinary shares within the period beginning one year before and ending three years after the disposal of the property.

The reinvestment is treated as the top slice of the gain. Thus Jane will only need to invest £44,096 in order to roll over the full amount of her gain.

The gain will become chargeable if:

- the shares are sold without being replaced
- Jane becomes non-UK resident
- within three years of the reinvestment, the company ceases to carry on a qualifying trade.

c) There are a number of investments producing tax-free income:

- National Savings Bank ordinary account – the first £70 of interest is free of tax, although the interest rate is generally low.
- National Savings Certificates are tax free. They must be held for five years. The maximum investment is generally £10,000.
- Save As You Earn schemes – a fixed sum of between £1 and £20 per month is invested over a five-year period. At the end of the period a tax-free bonus equivalent to 14 monthly payments is added. Alternatively, the funds can be left for a further two years, in which case the bonus will be doubled. However, on its own a SAYE scheme is not a viable proposition for the amount of funds Jane has available to invest.
- TESSAs – Tax Exempt Special Savings Accounts are offered by banks and building societies. A maximum of £9,000 can be invested over a five-year period: up to £3,000 in the first year and up to £1,800 in each subsequent year. The capital must remain untouched for the full five-year period, otherwise the account loses its tax-free status.
- Personal Equity Plan – up to £6,000 per fiscal year can be invested in a general PEP, plus up to £3,000 in a single company PEP. The plan manager invests the funds in ordinary shares of companies incorporated in the UK or EC. Some investment in unit or investment trusts is also permitted. The income arising on investments held within the plan is free of tax. There is no minimum period of time for which the PEP must be held.

d) i) Christine will not have to account for VAT on the income of her new business as a result of the partnership being registered, because the partnership is regarded as a separate entity for VAT purposes. Customs and Excise do have the power to aggregate the turnover of two separate businesses if they believe the businesses have been split in order to avoid VAT registration. However, here the two businesses concerned are completely different and do not involve the same staff or assets. Thus, as Christine's turnover is below the registration limit of £45,000 she will not have to account for VAT.

ii) If Christine registered voluntarily, she would have to absorb the VAT on 25% of her sales: £20,000 × 25% × 7/47 = £745. VAT could be added onto the price of the supplies made to the other 75% of the customers as they would be able to recover it.

Christine could then recover the following amounts of input tax suffered:

	£
Leasing (1,175 × 7/47)	175
Telephone (752 × 50% × 7/47)	56
Entertaining (non-deductible)	–
Insurance (exempt)	–
	231

The input tax recoverable is not sufficient to compensate for the output tax which Christine would have to absorb.

However, assuming Christine were to register within six months of incurring the pre-launch advertising expenditure, the input tax suffered on this expenditure would also be deductible: £3,525 × 7/47 = £525. Therefore, in the first year of trading, the input tax recoverable would just exceed the output tax suffered.

On balance it is probably not worth Christine registering voluntarily. However, before making her decision, Christine should also consider the prestige involved in being registered for VAT – it conceals the size of a small business – and the administration costs involved.

iii) As mentioned above, input tax incurred on services received within the six months preceding the commencement of trading is deductible. Therefore, for VAT purposes, there is no need to defer the pre-launch advertising expenditure.

For income tax purposes, the expenditure must be incurred within seven years of the commencement of trading and must be of a type which would be allowable under the normal Schedule D rules. The expenditure will then be treated as a loss incurred in the first year of assessment. Relief will be given once according to the normal loss relief rules.

Deferring pre-trading expenditure was always advisable under the old Schedule D commencement rules as it was then deductible in the first set of accounts. These first accounts were used as the basis for the first two or three years' assessments. Thus relief was obtained more than once.

Under the new current year basis of assessment, deferment is still beneficial; however, the benefit is effectively only a timing difference. Some of the profits of the first accounting period are likely to be assessed in both the first and second years of assessment, so initially relief will be obtained more than once. However, over the life of the business the profits will be taxed in full, once and once only, so this additional relief will effectively be reversed when overlap relief is given.

8 a) As Howard owns 50% of the shares in Howdon Limited, the market value of his shareholding at 31 March 1982 can be taken as 50% of the company's net assets at that date: £120,000 × 50% = £60,000.

No CGT liability will arise on the issue of shares in Aardvark plc, therefore, the only CGT liability will be in respect of the cash element of the consideration. This cash element amounts to 3/4 of the total consideration.

The gain arising on the disposal of the shares in Howdon Ltd is as follows:

	Cost	*March 1982*
	£	*£*
Disposal proceeds	150,000	150,000
Cost: £5,000 × 3/4	(3,750)	
March 1982: £60,000 × 3/4		(45,000)
Unindexed gain	146,250	105,000
Indexation: £45,000 × 0.811	(36,495)	(36,495)
Chargeable gain	109,755	68,505

The lower gain of £68,505 will be chargeable.

As Howard is aged over 55 and has been in business for more than ten years he is entitled to the maximum amount of retirement relief. This is the lower of (i) £250,000 and (ii) the gain relating to chargeable business assets:

	Chargeable assets	*Chargeable business assets*
	£	£
Goodwill	100,000	100,000
Freehold shops	175,000	175,000
Investment	16,000	–
	291,000	275,000

The shop fittings have been excluded because they are chattels each with a value of less than £6,000. The net current assets have been excluded because they are not chargeable to CGT.

The gain eligible for retirement relief is, therefore: £68,505 × 275,000/291,000 = £64,738. The balance of the gain (£68,505 – £64,738 = £3,767) remains chargeable but is covered by the annual exemption.

b) The gift of shares in Aardvark plc will be a chargeable disposal for CGT purposes. Howard is not entitled to retirement relief on this gain as the shares disposed of were not those of a personal company. Neither is he entitled to holdover relief because the shares are quoted.

The shares in Aardvark plc stand in the shoes of the Howdon Ltd shares. Their March 1982 value is therefore: £60,000 × 1/4 × 2,500/12,500 = £3,000. The original cost of the shares can be ignored as rebasing will clearly produce the lower gain:

	£
Disposal proceeds (2,500 × £4.50)	11,250
March 1982 value	(3,000)
Unindexed gain	8,250
Indexation: £3,000 × 0.826	(2,478)
Chargeable gain	5,772

If Howard makes this transfer during 1994/95, part of this gain will be chargeable: £5,772 – (5,800 – 3,767) = 3,739. The CGT due will be £1,496 (3,739 × 40%).

If Howard delays making this transfer until 1995/96, there will be no CGT due, as the gain is covered by the annual exemption.

The gift of shares in Aardvark plc is a potentially exempt transfer (PET) for IHT purposes. The value of the gift is £11,250.

£1,000 of the gift to Donald in consideration of his forthcoming marriage is exempt from IHT because Howard is his brother. The balance is a PET.

PETs only become chargeable if the donor dies within seven years of making the transfer. No tax is payable at the time the transfer is made.

The full gift of £2,000 to Oxfam is exempt because Oxfam is a recognised charity.

The cash of £50,000 settled into a discretionary trust is a chargeable lifetime transfer (CLT). The rate of IHT is 20% which is half the death rate in force at the date of the transfer. Howard should ensure that this is the first one of the transfers he makes during 1994/95 as it will then receive the benefit of two years annual exemptions. These exemptions would otherwise be allocated to the PETs if they were made first.

12

As Howard had made an earlier CLT, this will have utilised most of his nil rate band. Assuming he takes the above advice regarding the timing of his transfers, the IHT due will be:

	£
April 1993: £120,000 – (3,000 × 2)	114,000
March 1995: £50,000 – (3,000 × 2)	44,000
	158,000
Nil rate band	(150,000)
Chargeable	8,000
IHT due: £8,000 × 20/80 =	2,000

The loan to Howard's friend is at a market rate of interest, therefore there is no loss to the estate and no IHT is payable.

c) If Howard does not accept the offer of part-time employment his income tax liability for 1995/96 will be as follows:

	£	£
Pension (£200 × 52)		10,400
Loan interest (£20,000 × 10%)		2,000
Dividend (10,000 × 8p × 100/80)		1,000
BSI (£750 × 100/75)		1,000
Statutory total income		14,400
Age allowance	4,200	
Less: (14,400 – 14,200) × 1/2	(100)	(4,100)
Taxable		10,300
Tax payable: (3,000 + 1,000) × 20%		800
(10,300 – 4,000) × 25%		1,575
		2,375

(Note that the lower rate band has been extended by the dividend income, which is only taxable at 20%).

If Howard accepts the offer of part-time employment his income tax liability will increase as follows:

	£
Income (as before)	14,400
Schedule E (£600 × 12)	7,200
Statutory total income	21,600
Personal allowance (restricted)	(3,445)
Taxable	18,155
Tax payable: (3,000 + 1,000) × 20% =	800
(18,155 – 4,000) × 25% =	3,539
	4,339

By accepting the offer of part-time employment Howard will lose his entitlement to age allowance.

The marginal rate of tax due on Howard's earnings will be: (4,339 – 2,375)/7,200 = 27.3%.

9 a) The courts will consider the badges of trade:

- The subject matter of the transaction. Investments are usually purchased because they yield an income or give the owner personal enjoyment.
- The length of ownership. There is a presumption that assets held for a long time are investments (thus capital in nature), whereas trading generally involves selling assets within a short time of their acquisition.
- The frequency of similar transactions.
- Work done on the property, for example in order to make it more marketable.
- The way in which the asset was acquired.
- The circumstances responsible for its sale. The sale of assets in an emergency will probably not be classed as trading.
- The motive for the transaction.
- The courts may also consider the background of the taxpayer. If Mr Williams had been employed as a builder or a property developer, the courts would be more likely to conclude that he was trading in this instance.

b) Land is a difficult subject matter, as it is quite often held as an investment. In Mr Williams' case, had he just sold the property inherited from his father, it would have been very difficult for the General Commissioners to conclude that he was trading. However, the fact that he purchased additional land with the knowledge that there was a prospect of development, and the fact that he obtained planning permission and undertook work on the site, lead me to conclude that the Commissioners were right in their decision.

Note: Candidates who came to a different decision in part (b) could still pick up full marks provided that their reasoning was sensible and fully explained.

c) i) The tax due assuming this is a trading transaction is:

	£
Sale	155,000
Cost of sales	
(50,000 + 49,000 + 10,000)	(109,000)
Gross profit	46,000
Interest (30,000 × 10% × 16/12)	(4,000)
Schedule DI profit	42,000
Tax due: £42,000 × 40% =	16,800

ii) The tax due assuming this is a capital transaction is:

	£
Sale proceeds	155,000
Cost (50,000 + 49,000)	(99,000)
Enhancement expenditure	(10,000)
Unindexed gain	46,000
Indexation: £99,000 × 0.020	(1,980)
£10,000 × 0.001	(10)
	44,010
Annual exemption	(5,800)
Chargeable gain	38,210
Tax due: £38,210 × 40% =	15,284

(Note that the indexation due in respect of the drainage is computed according to the date of the payment.)

d) The normal due dates (NDD) for a 1993/94 schedule DI assessment are 1 January 1994 and 1 July 1994. As this assessment was issued late, however, its NDD is 30 days after the issue of the assessment: 3 July 1994.

The tax not postponed has an actual due date (ADD) 30 days after the Inspector's agreement to postpone: 2 September 1994.

The reckonable date for interest purposes is the middle one of three dates:

i) NDD	3 July 1994
ii) ADD	2 September 1994
iii) Table date	1 July 1994

Interest therefore runs from 3 July 1994 and the amount due is: £13,000 × 10% × 59/365 = £210.14

The tax postponed and found to be payable on appeal, has an ADD 30 days after the notice of determination was issued to Mr Williams: 3 February 1995.

The reckonable date for interest purposes is again the middle one of three dates:

i) NDD	3 July 1994
ii) ADD	3 February 1995
iii) Table date	1 July 1994

Interest again runs from 3 July 1994 and the amount due is: £3,800 × 10% × 212/365 = £220.71

Mr Williams will therefore have to pay total interest of £430.85 (210.14 + 220.71).

Note: When computing interest on overdue tax it is important to explain fully all of the stages that you have gone through in reaching your answer. Marks will be awarded for the correct procedure even if the final answer is incorrect.

10 a) i) A taxpayer has a right of appeal against an assessment if he believes it to be incorrect. In order to appeal, notice must be given to the Inspector, in writing, within 30 days of the issue of the assessment. In addition, a taxpayer can make an error or mistake claim in respect of figures included in his return. This claim must be made within six years of the end of the year of assessment concerned. The error may be one of fact or law. A claim is not permitted if the return was made in accordance with the general understanding of the law at that time. After such a claim, the normal appeals procedure applies.

ii) The Inspector could make an additional assessment in respect of 1993/94 if he 'discovers' that profits have not been assessed. 'Discovery' has a very wide meaning. It can cover the situation where the Inspector comes to the conclusion that there has been an under-assessment (due perhaps to a computational error) or simply changes his opinion. It does not necessarily require new facts to have come to light. However, discovery cannot be applied to matters which have been specifically considered in the determination of an appeal. The Inspector must normally make his discovery within six years of the end of the year of assessment concerned. If there has been fraud or neglect, this time limit can be extended to 20 years after the end of the year of assessment concerned.

b) i) A tax return should be completed within 30 days of the date of its issue. In practice, however, this time limit is not enforced. Even if the Inspector does not issue a return, Paul is still required to notify the Inspector of his chargeability to tax within one year of the end of the year of assessment concerned.

12

Failure to submit a return could result in the imposition of a penalty. The maximum penalty is £300 plus £60 for each day that the return remains outstanding after the imposition of the penalty. In addition, should the information not be provided by the end of the following year of assessment, the Revenue can impose a penalty based on the amount of CGT due. The maximum penalty is 100% although this will usually be mitigated.

ii) Hugh has the same obligations to report his gain to the Inspector. However, as his gain is covered by his annual exemption of £5,800 and the disposal proceeds do not exceed £11,600, he does not need to submit a calculation.

In Hugh's case, as no tax will be lost as a result of his failure to notify the Inspector, the maximum penalty that can be imposed is £100.

c) At present Barney makes the following profit:

	£
Turnover	40,000
Cost of sales (60%)	(24,000)
Gross profit (40%)	16,000

This cost of sales figure includes input tax of £3,574 (£24,000 × 7/47) which is currently irrecoverable as Barney is not VAT registered. If he were to register, this input tax would be recoverable.

As Barney retails to the general public, and as the market is highly competitive, it is unlikely that he will be able to add VAT onto the prices he currently charges. He will therefore have to meet the output tax himself: £40,000 × 7/47 = £5,957.

By registering for VAT Barney will therefore reduce his current gross profit by £2,383 (£5,957 – £3,574).

As the new customer is VAT registered, Barney will be able to add VAT onto the contract price of £10,000. The input tax suffered on his cost of sales will be recoverable, giving him a VAT-exclusive price of £10,000 × 60% × 40/47 = £5,106. The gross profit from taking on the new contract will be £4,894 (£10,000 – £5,106).

So it will be worthwhile for Barney to accept the new contract and register for VAT as his total gross profit will increase by £2,511 (£4,894 – £2,383).

Barney cannot avoid registering for VAT by setting up a new company. Although the company would be separate from Barney both legally and for the purpose of other taxes, Customs and Excise have the power, for VAT purposes, to aggregate the turnover of different businesses if it appears that they have been split in order to avoid registration.

11 a) In determining whether the principal private residence rules apply, periods prior to 31 March 1982 are ignored. Leigh was in actual occupation for the four years and six months covering the period 1 April 1982 to 30 September 1986. The two years between 1 October 1986 and 30 September 1988 cannot be deemed a period of occupation as Leigh never reoccupied the property. The gain accruing during the 33 months between 1 October 1988 and 30 June 1991 may be relieved by the letting exemption. The final 36 months of ownership are always exempt provided that the property has been the taxpayer's main residence at some point.

Leigh's chargeable gain has been computed using the March 1982 valuation as this will clearly give the lower gain:

	£	£
Disposal proceeds		140,000
March 1982 value	38,000	
Enhancement expenditure	12,000	(50,000)
Unindexed gain		90,000
Indexation: £38,000 × 0.801	30,438	
£12,000 × 0.508	6,096	(36,534)
Gain		53,466
Exempt as PPR: £53,466 × 90/147		(32,734)
Letting exemption, the lowest of:		
i) Maximum exemption	40,000	
ii) Gain re letting £53,466 × 33/147	12,003	
iii) Gain exempt as PPR	32,734	(12,003)
		8,729
Annual exemption		(5,800)
Chargeable gain		2,929

b) *House 1:*

	£
Rent due (£400 × 6)	2,400
Bad debts (£400 × 4)	(1,600)
Repairs	(1,500)
Loss	(700)

House 2:

Rent due (£350 × 5)	1,750

The structural repairs are not deductible as they relate to pre-ownership dilapidations.

Leasehold shop:

As Leigh paid a premium to acquire the lease, she is entitled to an additional deduction in computing the amount of premium assessable on her under Schedule A:

		£
Premium		5,000
Less: £5,000 × 2% × (4 – 1)		(300)
		4,700
Premium paid	10,000	
£10,000 × 2% × (10 – 1)	(1,800)	
Assessable on landlord	8,200	
Relief available £8,200 × 4/10 =		(3,280)
		1,420
Shop rent due		3,400
Less rent payable		(2,600)
		800

The loss on house 1 cannot be set against the profit on either house 2 or the shop because these are let on tenant's repairing lease.

As the flat is let on a landlord's repairing lease, Leigh could offset the loss on house 1 against the profit from the flat. However, this can only be done if an election is made to split the assessment of the flat between schedule A (in respect of the building) and schedule DVI (in respect of the contents). This election must be made by 5 April 1997. The election will result in the following assessments:

	Schedule A	Schedule DVI
	£	£
Rents	3,380	1,300
Insurance	(150)	(250)
Wear and tear (4,680 × 10%)	–	(468)
	3,230	582

Leigh's net assessments are therefore:

Schedule A:	£	£
Flat	3,230	
Loss on house 1	(700)	2,530
House 2		1,750
Shop rent		800
Premium		1,420
		6,500
Schedule DVI:		582

c) i) In order to be classed as a furnished holiday letting, a letting must be on a commercial basis with a view to the realisation of profit and:

- ▶ must be available for letting at least 140 days during the fiscal year
- ▶ must be actually let for at least 70 days
- ▶ must not normally be in the same occupation for more than 31 days, during a period of seven months including the 70 days referred to above.

ii) Provided the above conditions are met, the following benefits will accrue:

- ▶ the income is classed as earned income
- ▶ the tax is payable in two equal instalments on 1 January in the year of assessment and 1 July in the following year
- ▶ personal pension premiums may be provided for out of the income
- ▶ losses are treated as trading losses
- ▶ the property is treated as a business asset and retirement relief, rollover relief and gift relief may be claimed in respect of any capital gains
- ▶ capital allowances are available for plant and machinery
- ▶ any expenses allowable under schedule DI are deductible in computing the amount assessable (eg, interest payments will be allowed as an expense rather than as a charge)
- ▶ relief is available for pre-trading expenditure.

12 a) The first proposal is to appoint Gabrielle as an employee on 6 April 1994 and give the entire business to her on 5 April 2000. This will have the following consequences:

- ▶ If Charles survives until 5 April 2000 and gifts the business to Gabrielle a capital gain will arise. As Charles will be over 55, he will be able to make a claim for retirement relief. As he will have owned the business for more than 10 years he will be eligible for the full relief. The first £250,000 of gains relating to business assets will be completely tax free. This should easily cover Charles' gains.
- ▶ Retirement relief is only available in respect of business assets. As one-fifth of the shop has been let out this will not qualify as a business asset. The gain relating to this part of the shop will be £8,000 (40,000 × 1/5). The majority of

12

this gain will be covered by Charles' annual exemption. Holdover relief is not available as this part of the shop is a non-business asset.

- If Charles survives until 5 April 2000, the proposed gift of the business will be a PET. As it is likely he will die within three years of the transfer no taper relief will be due. The gift will, however, be valued at the time of transfer rather than the date of death and its value will be further reduced by two annual exemptions of £3,000 each.
- Gabrielle will be liable for the inheritance tax due if the PET becomes chargeable as a result of death. She will be entitled to business property relief (see later) provided that she has not disposed of the business.
- If Charles dies before gifting the business to Gabrielle, it will form part of his estate on death. His business assets will qualify for 100% business property relief. At current values the inheritance tax payable will be as follows:

	£
Shop (240,000 × 1/5)	48,000
Private residence	140,000
	188,000
Less nil rate band	(150,000)
	38,000

Inheritance tax due: £38,000 × 40% = £15,200

- The net current assets, 4/5 of the shop and any goodwill are all covered by 100% business property relief. No capital gains arise on death.

The second proposal is to make an immediate gift of the entire business to Gabrielle on 6 April 1994. This will have the following consequences:

- As above, a capital gain will arise on the lifetime transfer of the business. Retirement relief will be available as although Charles is not actually retiring, he is ceasing to have any interest in the assets of the business.
- As above, the lifetime transfer of the business will be a PET. Although Charles will still be involved in the business the transfer does not constitute a gift with reservation as the profit sharing is a commercial arrangement.
- Charles may survive for seven years after making the gift, in which case the transfer will be free of inheritance tax.
- Charles should survive for a minimum of three years after making the gift, therefore taper relief will be available.
- As above, by making a lifetime transfer, two years' annual exemptions will be obtained and the gift will be valued at the time of transfer rather than at the date of death.
- Business property relief will again be available to Gabrielle provided that she has not disposed of the business prior to Charles' death.
- On death, Charles' estate will only consist of his private residence, which is valued below the nil rate band, so no IHT will be payable.

12

b) i) At present the taxable incomes of Gabrielle and Keith are as follows:

	Gabrielle	Keith
	£	£
Schedule E	20,000	40,000
Dividends (£2,500 × 100/80)	–	3,125
Building society interest (£6,000 × 100/75)	–	8,000
	20,000	51,125
Personal allowance	(3,445)	(3,445)
Taxable income	16,555	47,680

At present Keith is liable to tax at 40%, whereas Gabrielle is not utilising her full basic rate band. It is therefore necessary to transfer income from one spouse to the other. In order to transfer income, capital must also be transferred.

The first priority should be to transfer the shares to Gabrielle. Assuming she remains a basic rate taxpayer, the dividends will only be liable to tax at 20% instead of 40% as at present. The building society account should be put into joint names, and the interest shared equally. This will enable Gabrielle to stay just within the basic rate band.

Relief for the married couple's allowance and the mortgage interest is now given by means of a tax credit rather than by a deduction in computing taxable income. As both of these reliefs are restricted to the lower rate of tax, their allocation will have no effect on the couple's overall income tax liability.

ii) At present, no inheritance tax would be payable on the death of the first spouse as the exemption for transfers between spouses would apply. However, neither spouse is utilising their nil rate band and this will lead to increased inheritance tax on the death of the second spouse. Both Gabrielle and Keith should change their wills so that an amount equivalent to the nil rate band (currently £150,000) is left to their children.

It is therefore necessary to ensure that each spouse has an estate of at least £150,000. After making the transfers necessary to reduce the couple's income tax liability, the estates are as follows:

	Gabrielle	Keith
	£	£
Jewellery	80,000	–
Shares	50,000	–
House (150,000 – 50,000)	50,000	50,000
Building society deposits	50,000	50,000
	230,000	100,000

As the income-producing assets cannot be transferred back to Keith without affecting the income tax liability, the only transferable assets are the house and the jewellery. By transferring the jewellery, Keith's estate will become £180,000, while Gabrielle's estate will be reduced to £150,000, which equates to the current nil rate band.

Note that Gabrielle's estate will be increased by the transfer of the business from Charles. However, this will be covered by business property relief, with the exception of 1/5 of the value of the shop.

12

13 a) *Jimmy Corkhill – Statutory total income 1994/95*

	£
Schedule E – Director's remuneration (6 × 4,000)	24,000
Schedule D – Partnership share	18,000
Schedule A – Shop 1 (£2,000 × 2)	4,000
– Shop 2 (loss of £900 unrelieved)	–
Dividend from Light plc (20,000 × 6p × 100/80)	1,500
Trust income:	
Interest in possession trust	
(30,000 × 6p × 100/80) – (£1,500 × 6/12)	1,500
Discretionary trust (£1,625 × 100/65)	2,500
Statutory total income	51,500

No relief is available in respect of the mortgage interest paid by Jimmy since it is not in respect of his main residence.

The loss on the second shop cannot be set against the rent from the first shop as they are both let under tenant's repairing leases. No carry forward is possible due to the change of landlord.

b) *Jimmy Corkhill – Inheritance tax computation 5 October 1994*

Free estate

	£	£
Personalty		
Light plc shares 20,000 × 193p		38,600
Units in Rapide trust 2,000 × 110p		2,200
Partnership share (see notes)		100,000
		140,800
Less: Income tax due	9,000	
Funeral expenses (half)	1,500	
		10,500
		130,300
Realty		
Freehold property – Main residence	290,000	
Flat (see notes)	90,000	
Shops (2 × 75,000)	150,000	
Villa (100,000/4)	25,000	
		555,000
Net free estate		685,300
Settled property		
Interest in possession (see notes) (57,900 – 30,000)		27,900
Chargeable estate		713,200
Less nil rate band		150,000
Chargeable at 40%		563,200
Inheritance tax payable: £563,200 × 40% =		225,280

Estate rate: (225,280/713,200 × 100) = 31.59%

Double tax relief of £3,750 will be due being the lower of:

i) 15,000/4 = £3,750
ii) 25,000 × 31.59% = £7,897

IHT of £221,530 (225,280 – 3,750 DTR) will be due from the estate, of which £115,303 ((290,000 + 75,000) × 31.59%) can be paid by instalments. This option is not available in respect of the property that was subsequently sold. Interest on the unpaid balance of IHT due by instalments will be added to each instalment. IHT of £8,813 (27,900 × 31.59%) will be due from the trust. The IHT not payable by instalments will be due on 30 April 1995. The IHT payable by instalments will be due in ten equal annual amounts commencing on 30 April 1995.

Notes

The agreement made by the partners is classed as a contract for sale. The existence of such a contract means that business property relief is not available.

The flat is presumed to be held equally between Jimmy and his wife. Since the mortgage would have been cleared as a result of Jimmy's death, it is not deducted from the value of the flat.

The total value of the trust is £57,900 (30,000 × 193p). Jimmy's share is the value remaining after setting aside an amount equal to the capital value of the annuity. The annuity's capital value is the lower of:

i) £57,900 × 1,500/2,250 = £38,600
£2,250 represents the trust's annual income (30,000 × 6p × 100/80).

ii) £57,900 × 1,500/2,895 = £30,000
£2,895 represents the estimated annual income based on the FT actuaries all share index (£57,900 × 5%).

c) i) It would be beneficial for the executors of Jimmy's estate to elect to substitute the sale proceeds for the death value of land and buildings sold within four years of death, because this would reduce Jimmy's chargeable estate by £15,000. The flat was sold at a loss of £10,000 (a half share of £20,000) and the villa at a loss of £5,000 [25,000 – (100,000/5)]. The subsequent sales by Billy are ignored. Jimmy's IHT liability would be reduced by £6,000 (£15,000 × 40%).

ii) It would be possible for Billy to make a deed of family arrangement so that some, or all, of his brother's property passes directly to his children. This could be done by way of a trust until they become adults. There would be no IHT saving on Jimmy's death, but this property would not then suffer a further IHT charge upon Billy's death.

It should also be noted that if no deed of family arrangement was to be made and Billy died within five years of Jimmy, then quick succession relief would mitigate the IHT liability.

14 a) i) A transfer into an accumulation and maintenance trust is a potentially exempt transfer (PET) for IHT purposes. Assuming that Edna survives for seven years after making the transfer, there will be no IHT liability. If she dies within seven years of making the transfer, IHT will be due. The IHT will be based on the value of the shares at the time of the transfer. The IHT will be reduced by taper relief if Edna has survived for at least three years. The IHT will be borne by the trustees. The maximum IHT due, assuming the nil rate band remains at the 1994/95 amount, will be:

	£
Value of transfer	200,000
Less annual exemptions: £3,000 × 2	(6,000)
	194,000
Nil rate band	(150,000)
Chargeable	44,000
IHT due: £44,000 × 40%	17,600

12

Edna will be liable to CGT on the gain of £40,000 less the annual exemption of £5,800. The tax will be calculated at Edna's marginal rate. Holdover relief cannot be claimed because the transfer is neither immediately chargeable to IHT nor the transfer of a business asset.

ii) A transfer into a discretionary trust is a chargeable lifetime transfer for IHT purposes. The IHT due by Edna is: Chargeable transfer (as before) £44,000 × 20/80 = £11,000.

If Edna should die within seven years of making the transfer, the tax due will need to be recomputed using the full death rate of 40%. The gross transfer for this calculation will be £205,000 (194,000 + 11,000). This additional tax will be payable by the trustees. Taper relief may again be due if Edna survives for at least three years.

For CGT purposes, Edna can claim holdover relief because this transfer is immediately chargeable to IHT. The gain of £40,000 will thus be deducted from the base cost of the shares acquired by the trustees.

b) i) An accumulation and maintenance trust is a privileged form of discretionary trust. As a result no IHT arises on the distribution of the assets to the beneficiaries.

For CGT purposes, a distribution of assets is a chargeable disposal. The assets will be deemed to be disposed of at their market values. The trustees will therefore have to pay tax at the rate of 35% on any gains after the deduction of an annual exemption of £2,900.

Holdover relief is not due as the shares are not qualifying business property and neither is there an immediate charge to IHT.

ii) The transfer of property from a discretionary trust will incur liability to an exit charge, calculated as follows:

	£
Initial value of trust property	200,000
Less nil rate band	(150,000)
Chargeable	50,000

Notional IHT due: £50,000 × 20% = £10,000

Rate of tax on notional transfer: 10,000/200,000 = 5%

Rate of exit charge tax: 5% × 30% = 1.5%

The exit charge due is therefore:

£200,000 × 1.5% × 20/40 = £1,500

A chargeable gain arises on the disposal of the trust property. As the disposal is immediately chargeable to IHT, holdover relief may be claimed.

c) As the gift of the clock is in consideration of marriage it will qualify for an exemption of £5,000. The balance of £2,500 is a potentially exempt transfer. It will only become chargeable to IHT if Edna dies within seven years of making the gift.

The clock is a non-wasting chattel. The gain arising on its disposal is:

	£
Deemed disposal proceeds	7,500
Cost	(2,500)
Unindexed gain	5,000
Indexation: £5,000 × 0.476	(2,380)
Chargeable gain	2,620

The gain is subject to marginal relief. It will thus be restricted to a maximum of: (7,500 – 6,000) × 5/3 = £2,500.

The gift of the agricultural land to Nelson is a chargeable disposal for CGT purposes. It will give rise to the following gain:

	£
Deemed disposal proceeds	200,000
Cost	(50,000)
Unindexed gain	150,000
Indexation: £50,000 × 0.738	(36,900)
Chargeable gain	113,100

Letting the land does not constitute a business, so Edna cannot claim either retirement relief or gift relief.

The gift of the land is a PET for IHT purposes. No IHT will be due unless Edna dies within seven years of making the transfer. If Edna does die within seven years, agricultural property relief may be due as Edna has owned the land for more than seven years. As the land was transferred with vacant possession, the rate of relief would be 100%. Relief is only available in respect of the agricultural value of £120,000. In addition, relief will only be available if Nelson continues to own the property, and the land is still agricultural property, at the date of Edna's death. Business property relief is not available because, as previously mentioned, letting the land does not constitute a business.

15 Jones Ltd

Alternative loss relief claims

a) As Jones Ltd's confectionery business is due to cease at the end of 1993, the company cannot carry the loss forward under s393(1) as it will have no future profits of the same trade.

b) Jones Ltd could claim relief for the loss under s393A. This will involve firstly relieving the loss against profits of the same accounting period, before the deduction of any charges. The balance of the loss can then be carried back against profits of the preceding 36 months on a last in, first out basis. Profits for these purposes are before the deduction of non-trading charges. A claim for relief under s393A must be made by 31 December 1996.

A claim under s393A would give relief as follows:

	30/9/91	*30/9/92*	*31/12/92*	*31/12/93*	*31/12/94*
	£	£	£	£	£
Sched DI	57,000	45,000	7,000	30,000	–
Sched A	–	24,000	6,000	24,000	24,000
CG	11,000	–	–	–	–
	68,000	69,000	13,000	54,000	24,000
s393A	(51,000)	(49,800)	(13,000)	(34,800)	(24,000)
	17,000	19,200	–	19,200	–
Deb int	(9,600)	(19,200)	–	(19,200)	–
Deed	(6,000)	–	–	–	–
PCTCT	1,400	–	–	–	–

Note the s393A claim for the year ended 30 September 1991 is £68,000 × 9/12 = £51,000. However, the Revenue's view is that the apportionment of profits should be after the deduction of trade charges. This approach would give loss relief of: (68,000 – 9,600) × 9/12 = £43,800.

Relief for the last four non-trading charges would be lost.

If the Inland Revenue will accept a terminal loss claim, the 1994 trading charge of £19,200 may be added to the loss carried back.

c) Jones Ltd could surrender part of its loss to a 75% subsidiary under s402. Tom Ltd is only a 60% subsidiary and thus could not claim any of the loss under this provision. Jerry Ltd, however, could claim part of the loss as Jones Ltd holds an effective interest of 70% + (30 × 60%) = 88%. As Jerry Ltd only joined the Jones Ltd group part way through Jones Ltd's accounting period, its profits will need to be time-apportioned in determining the amount of loss which may be relieved in this way: £10,000 × 9/12 = £7,500. A claim under s402 must be made by 31 December 1996.

d) Tom Ltd is a consortium owned company as more than 75% of its share capital is held by Jones Ltd and Minor Ltd, both of which are UK resident companies, and neither of which holds less than 5% of Tom Ltd's ordinary share capital. Jones Ltd could surrender losses of £12,000 (£20,000 × 60%) to Tom Ltd provided that the consent of Tom and Minor is received. This claim must be made by 31 December 1996.

e) Jones Ltd is in receipt of franked investment income each year, which regularly exceeds its franked payments. If it makes a claim under s393A it could then make a further claim under s242. This claim would result in a repayment of the ACT suffered on the surplus franked investment income.

The maximum amount claimable under s242 is:

	30/9/91	*30/9/92*	*31/12/92*	*31/12/93*	*31/12/94*
	£	£	£	£	£
FII	20,000	20,000	–	20,000	18,750
FP	10,000	10,000	–	–	–
	10,000	10,000	–	20,000	18,750
FII c/f	10,000	–	–	–	–
FII b/f	–	10,000	–	–	–
s242 claim	–	–	–	20,000	18,750
Repayment due: 25%/20%	–	–	–	5,000	3,750

A claim under this section normally only results in a cash flow advantage as the relief reverses when a subsequent dividend is paid. The claim has the same time limits as a s393A claim.

Summary

As all of the companies concerned are liable to tax at the small companies rate, a tax saving of 25% will result from any loss relief claims made (with the exception of the s242 claim). Jones Ltd's loss is sufficient to make all of the above claims.

16 a) Apricot's adjusted Schedule DI loss for its final accounting period is as follows:

	£
Net loss per accounts	(76,000)
Depreciation	16,000
Debenture interest	5,000
Charitable deed	1,000
Redundancy payments	10,000
Professional fees	2,000
Balancing allowances	(45,000)
Adjusted loss	(87,000)

The statutory redundancy payments are deductible. In addition, as the trade is ceasing, up to three times the statutory payment is deductible. The disallowance in respect of each employee is therefore £2,000 (10,000 – 2,000 – 6,000).

The professional fees have been disallowed as they are capital in nature.

As Apricot Ltd is ceasing to trade, this loss can be increased by the unrelieved trading charges of £5,000, giving a total loss of £92,000.

Under s393A ICTA 1988, the loss can be carried back against the total profits of the preceding 36 months as follows:

Year ended	31/3/91	31/3/92	31/3/93	31/3/94
	£	£	£	£
DI profits	60,000	26,000	29,000	7,000
Capital gains (19 – 8)	–	11,000	–	–
	60,000	37,000	29,000	7,000
s393A	–	(27,000)	(19,000)	–
	60,000	10,000	10,000	7,000
Debenture interest	(10,000)	(10,000)	(10,000)	(7,000)
Charitable deed	(1,000)	–	–	–
PCTCT	49,000	–	–	–
Corporation tax at 25%	12,250			
ACT (15,000 × 25/75)	(5,000)			
ACT carried back (7,500 × 25/75)	(2,500)			
MCT	4,750			

As a result of the loss relief claim, tax refunds will be due as follows:

Year ended 31/3/91 – £2,500 due to ACT being carried back.

Year ended 31/3/92 – £4,000. Prior to loss relief the figure of PCTCT was £26,000 (37,000 – 11,000 charges). Mainstream corporation tax was £4,000 ((26,000 × 25%) – £2,500 ACT). All of this will be repaid as a result of the loss relief claim.

Year ended 31/3/93 – £4,500. Prior to loss relief the figure of PCTCT was £18,000 (29,000 – 11,000 charges). All of the corporation tax paid will be repaid as a result of the loss relief claim (£18,000 × 25% = £4,500).

The following amounts will remain unrelieved:

- ▶ trading loss of £46,000 (92,000 – 19,000 – 27,000)
- ▶ trade charge of £3,000 (10,000 – 7,000) for the year ended 31 March 1994
- ▶ non-trade charges of £1,000 for the years ended 31 March 1992, 1993 and 1994, and the period ended 30 September 1994
- ▶ capital losses of £15,000 arising in the period ended 30 September 1994.

b) Both Melon Ltd and Plum Ltd will have capital gains as a result of the liquidation of Apricot Ltd:

	£
Disposal proceeds (150,000 × 40%)	60,000
Cost	(40,000)
Unindexed gain	20,000
Indexation £40,000 × $\frac{144.4 - 125.1}{125.1}$	(6,171)
Capital gain	13,829

Apricot Ltd is a consortium-owned company as more than 75% of its ordinary share capital is held by UK-resident companies, none of which owns less than 5%. A claim can therefore be made under s402 ICTA 1988 to group relieve Apricot Ltd's trading losses and unrelieved charges of the final accounting period.

The s402 claim should be made prior to the s393A claim as it will enable a greater proportion of the loss to be group relieved. The losses available for group relief are:

	£
Trading losses	92,000
Deed of covenant (period to 30/9/94)	1,000
	93,000

Plum Ltd must utilise its own current year loss prior to claiming any group relief.

The profits chargeable to corporation tax for both companies will be:

	Melon Ltd	Plum Ltd
	£	£
Schedule DI	110,000	–
Schedule DIII	10,000	–
Capital gain	13,829	13,829
	133,829	13,829
s393A	–	(8,000)
	133,829	5,829
Trade charges	(30,000)	–
	103,829	5,829
s402 (see below)	(37,200)	(2,915)
PCTCT	66,629	2,914
Corporation tax at 25%	16,657	728

The s402 claim is restricted to each consortium member's respective shareholding. Thus the maximum claim by both Melon Ltd and Plum Ltd is £37,200 (93,000 × 40%).

In addition, losses may only be group relieved against profits of a corresponding accounting period. It is therefore necessary to time-apportion the consortium members' profits as follows:

Melon Ltd £103,829 × 6/12 = £51,915

Plum Ltd £5,829 × 6/12 = £2,915

Note that Apricot Ltd's loss is sufficient to make all of the above claims.

c) As Apricot Ltd is a consortium-owned company, it is possible to make a group income election so that dividends could be paid to both Melon Ltd and Plum Ltd without accounting for ACT. If a group income election was not made, Apricot Ltd would probably find itself left with surplus ACT as, after claiming relief for its loss, it only has profits chargeable to corporation tax for the year ended 31 March 1991.

The payment of a dividend would reduce the proceeds paid out on liquidation. This would have the effect of reducing the capital gains arising to both Melon Ltd and Plum Ltd. The optimum amount of total dividend would be £34,572 (13,829 × 100/40) as this will reduce the capital gains to nil. The profits chargeable to corporation tax would also be reduced accordingly. However, this would result in Plum Ltd losing its claim to group relief.

17 a) i) A group for CGT purposes includes a parent company and its 75% subsidiaries. Subsubsidiaries may also be included provided that the principal company holds an effective interest of more than 50%. All group companies must be UK resident.

H, A and B form a CGT group. B is included because H's effective interest is (76% × 80%) + 5% = 65.8%.

C must be excluded as H's effective interest is less than 50%: (76% × 80% × 75%) + (5% × 75%) + 0.1 = 49.45%.

B and C cannot form a separate group as a company cannot be a member of two CGT groups.

ii) The transferor is treated as if it were transferring a fixed asset. The transfer is therefore on a no gain, no loss basis. The transferee is then deemed to appropriate the fixed asset to its trading stock. A chargeable gain will therefore arise to the transferee, based on the difference between the asset's market value and its no gain, no loss price plus any further indexation due. The asset will be included in the transferee's cost of sales figure at its market value.

iii) The transferee could elect to reduce the market value at the time of the appropriation by the amount of the chargeable gain (or increase it by the amount of any allowable loss). This will affect the schedule DI profit or loss when the asset is sold. Such an election would be favourable if the deemed disposal gave rise to a capital loss which could not be immediately relieved against chargeable gains. The capital loss would be transformed into a schedule DI expense, thus receiving immediate relief. Alternatively, if the deemed disposal gave rise to a gain, the company may prefer this to be a trading profit so as to receive an automatic set off of any trading losses.

12

b) i) Trading losses may be transferred between members of a 75% group. The definition differs from that used for CGT purposes because the effective interest of the principal company must be at least 75%.

H and A are members of the same group. B must be excluded as H's effective interest is only 65.8%. Unlike CGT groups, a company can be a member of more than one group, therefore, A and B can be members of a group. B and C can be members of a separate group.

Trading losses may also be transferred between a consortium owned company and members of the consortium. D is a consortium owned company as more than 75% of its ordinary share capital is owned by H, P and Q, the members of the consortium. To be a member of a consortium, each company must own more than 5%, but less than 75%, of D's share capital.

ii) Losses can only be transferred for a corresponding accounting period. In the case of a 75% group, the loss making company can surrender as much or as little of its loss as it wishes. The claimant company can only receive an amount equivalent to its profits chargeable to corporation tax after taking account of all losses of its own, with the exception of losses carried back under s393A.

In the case of a consortium, if a member of a consortium wishes to transfer its loss to the consortium owned company (COC), the transfer is limited to the amount of the COC's chargeable profits, equivalent to the percentage of ordinary share capital held by the consortium member.

If the COC wishes to surrender its loss to a member of the consortium, its loss is first deemed to be reduced by any possible s393A claim against its own current year profits. The transfer is then limited to the amount of the COC's remaining loss which is equivalent to the percentage of ordinary share capital owned by that consortium member.

iii) If Q was not resident in the UK, D Ltd would not fall within the definition of a consortium owned company and it would not be able to take part in any surrender of trading losses.

If A was not resident in the UK it could not form part of a 75% group for either CGT or trading loss purposes. The only group in existence for either purpose would then be B and C.

c) i) Dividends may be paid without accounting for ACT if they are paid between members of a 51% group. Thus H, A and B could all make a group income election. C could not be included in this election as H's effective interest is less than 50%. However, C could pay dividends to B without accounting for ACT.

Dividends may also be paid from a consortium owned company to members of a consortium without accounting for ACT. Thus D could pay dividends to H, P and Q under a group income election.

ii) A cash flow benefit results from making the election as the paying company is only required to account for ACT on dividends paid to minorities. This cash flow benefit is only temporary as the company's mainstream corporation tax liability will be increased. The election could, however, avoid the problem of a subsidiary having surplus ACT.

18 a) i) Dr Choler will be obtaining the shares in Envy Ltd at an undervalue. As he is the managing director of Grudge Ltd he will be assessable under Schedule E on the difference between the market value of the shares and the consideration paid, i.e. £50,000.

As Dr Choler is purchasing the whole of the shares in Envy Ltd, the company will be a close company. Interest paid on the loan to acquire ordinary shares in a close company will qualify as a charge because Dr Choler will control more than 5% of the ordinary share capital. There is no maximum amount of loan.

If all or part of the loan is written off an assessment will be made under Schedule F in the year in which the write off occurs. The sum assessable will be the amount released, grossed up at the lower rate of income tax. Dr Choler will have to account for additional tax based on the difference between the higher and lower rates of income tax.

ii) Relief for the unused trading losses will continue to be available irrespective of the change in ownership provided that there is no major change in the nature or conduct of the company's trade. Assuming that this condition remains satisfied for three years, the losses may be carried forward indefinitely against future trading profits.

Relief should be available for the redundancy costs as the trade is continuing. This relief will increase Envy Ltd's losses.

Envy Ltd will be a close company, therefore any loans it makes to Dr Choler (who is a participator) will oblige it to pay tax at the ACT rate to the Inland Revenue. This tax is not ACT and is not deductible in arriving at the company's MCT. If Dr Choler repays the loan, the Revenue will repay the tax. If the loan is written off, the tax will be forfeited. These provisions are excluded for loans not exceeding £15,000 to individuals who work full-time for the company and who do not have a material interest (5% of the ordinary shares) in the company. This exclusion will not apply to any loan to Dr Choler as he will hold all the share capital.

iii) The sale of the shares to Dr Choler will give rise to a CGT liability. The current market value will be used instead of the sale proceeds as the sale is between connected persons. The gain will be calculated as follows:

	Cost	*Rebased*
	£	£
Disposal proceeds	250,000	250,000
Cost/March 1982 value	(40,000)	(100,000)
Unindexed gain	210,000	150,000
Indexation: £100,000 × 0.806	(80,600)	(80,600)
	129,400	69,400

Indexation: $\frac{143.5 - 79.44}{79.44} = 0.806$

The lower gain of £69,400 will be chargeable.

Envy Ltd transferred an asset to Ire Ltd prior to leaving the group. No gain will arise on Envy Ltd leaving the group as the asset remains within the group.

b) Where companies are registered as a group for VAT purposes, VAT is not charged on transactions between companies in the group. Each group member is jointly and severally liable for the group's VAT liability. Envy Ltd's leaving the group will result in transactions between Envy Ltd and group members being liable to VAT.

Exports are zero-rated, therefore Envy Ltd is likely to be claiming repayments of VAT. In these circumstances Envy Ltd should apply to have a monthly tax period instead of a quarterly tax period. This will enable it to receive regular repayments which will aid the cash flow position.

19 a) The Finance Act 1982 sets out the following conditions which must be met before a company's purchase of its own shares qualifies for special treatment:

- The company must be an unquoted trading company.
- The share purchase must be wholly or mainly for the benefit of the trade, for example because a dissident shareholder is having an adverse effect on the running of the business.
- The vendor must be resident and ordinarily resident in the UK when the shares are purchased.
- The vendors or their spouses must have owned the shares throughout the five years preceding the date of purchase.
- The vendor's interest must be reduced by at least 25% as a result of the purchase.
- After the purchase, the vendor must cease to be connected with the company. Connected means owning (with associates) more than 30% of the issued ordinary share capital.

b) i) If the purchase does not qualify for the special treatment, then an amount equivalent to the sale proceeds less the original cost will be treated as a distribution.

Bliss Ltd will be required to account for ACT of (600,000 – 30,000) × 20/80 = £142,500. This must be paid under the quarterly accounting system by 14 April 1995. The ACT will be deductible in computing the company's mainstream corporation tax in the usual way.

As the company's profits are £200,000 p.a., it will not be able to offset all of this ACT during its accounting period ended 31 March 1995. The maximum set off is an amount equivalent to the company's chargeable profits multiplied by the ACT rate: £200,000 × 20% = £40,000. The distribution will therefore generate surplus ACT. As the company has not been paying any dividends, it will be possible to carry back this surplus ACT. It can be carried back on a last in, first out basis for a maximum of six years, subject to the maximum set off in each year. Carrying back the ACT will generate repayments of corporation tax from earlier periods.

Bluebeard will be in receipt of Schedule F income of (600,000 – 30,000) × 100/80 = £712,500 for 1994/95. The Inland Revenue will raise a taxed income assessment and Bluebeard will be required to pay additional income tax of £712,500 × (40% – 20%) = £142,500 by 1 December 1995.

ii) If the purchase does qualify for the special treatment, then it will be treated as a disposal for CGT purposes, rather than as a distribution.

There will be no ACT implications for Bliss Ltd.

12

Bluebeard will have a chargeable gain:

	£
Disposal proceeds	600,000
Cost	(30,000)
Unindexed gain	570,000
Indexation: £30,000 × 0.500	(15,000)
Chargeable gain	555,000

As Bluebeard is over 55 years old, has owned more than 5% of the share capital of Bliss Ltd, which is an unquoted trading company, and has worked full-time as a director of the company, he will be entitled to claim retirement relief. His qualifying period is nine years, therefore he will be entitled to full exemption for the first £225,000 (250,000 × 90%) of his gains. The balance of his gains up to £900,000 (1,000,000 × 90%) will be half exempt:

	£	£
Chargeable gain		555,000
Retirement relief:		
225,000 × 100% =	225,000	
(555,000 – 225,000) × 50% =	165,000	(390,000)
Chargeable gain		165,000
Annual exemption		(5,800)
Taxable		159,200
Tax due: £159,200 × 40% =		63,680

This CGT will be due on 1 December 1995.

c) For accounting periods ending after 30 September 1993, repayment supplement is calculated from the material date until the date the repayment order is issued. The material date is the later of (i) the date the tax was paid and (ii) the date on which the tax became due and payable. Corporation tax is normally due nine months after the end of the accounting period. Thus the material date for the accounting year ended 31 March 1995 is 1 January 1996.

Where surplus ACT is carried back to earlier periods not falling wholly within the preceding 12 months, the repayment is treated as being in respect of the accounting period in which the ACT was paid. A repayment in respect of the accounting year ended 31 March 1993 will only therefore attract repayment supplement if made after 1 January 1996. However, a repayment in respect of the accounting year ended 31 March 1994 will attract repayment supplement if it is made after 1 January 1995, as this accounting period falls within the 12 months immediately preceding 31 March 1995.

20 a) As Octopus Ltd owns more than 10% of the ordinary share capital of Dolmus Inc, the overseas dividend must be grossed up to take account of the underlying tax suffered. Grossing up in respect of withholding tax produces a figure of: £6,300 × 100/90 = £7,000. Grossing up again for underlying tax produces a figure of: £7,000 × 100/70 = £10,000.

12

The mainstream corporation tax due is as follows:

	Total	*UK*	*Overseas*
	£	*£*	*£*
Schedule DI	1,600,000	1,600,000	–
Schedule DV	10,000	–	10,000
	1,610,000	1,600,000	10,000
Charges	(30,000)	(30,000)	–
PCTCT	1,580,000	1,570,000	10,000
CT at 33%	521,400	518,100	3,300
DTR (see below)	(3,300)	–	(3,300)
ACT (see below)	(314,000)	(314,000)	–
MCT	204,100	204,100	–

Double tax relief is limited to the lower of:

i) the UK tax due: £10,000 × 33% = 3,300
ii) the overseas tax suffered: £10,000 – 6,300 = 3,700

The amount of ACT paid during the year was £465,000 × 20/80 = £116,250. This, together with the surplus ACT of £200,000 brought forward, gives a total of £316,250 available for set-off.

The maximum set-off of ACT is computed in respect of each source of income. The maximum set-off in respect of the UK income is £1,570,000 × 20% = £314,000. No set-off is possible in respect of the overseas income as the UK tax due on that source is extinguished by the credit relief claim.

Octopus Ltd therefore has surplus ACT of £2,250 available to carry forward. Note that if Octopus Ltd had elected to pay a dividend out of its foreign source profits, it could have claimed a repayment of any surplus ACT arising as a result of its Foreign Income Dividend (FID).

b) i) If the establishment is set up as a branch, any losses that it makes will automatically be combined with the profits or losses of the UK business. Thus there will be no need to make a claim in respect of any losses incurred by the Rubeenian branch.

The fact that the UK company may sell goods to the Rubeenian branch at an undervalue has no effect for corporation tax purposes.

As the Rubeenian branch will be regarded as part of Octopus Ltd, Octopus Ltd will be able to claim capital allowances in respect of any equipment purchased by the Rubeenian branch. The fact that such equipment will be situated overseas is irrelevant.

If the Rubeenian branch makes profits, all of these profits will be chargeable to UK corporation tax, irrespective of how much of the profits are actually remitted to the UK.

ii) If the establishment is set up as a subsidiary, it will be regarded as a completely separate company. It will be associated with Octopus Ltd and will thus share the small companies upper and lower limits. As Octopus Ltd is already chargeable at the standard rate of corporation tax, this change will have no impact on the amount of corporation tax payable by Octopus Ltd. Any losses made by the Rubeenian subsidiary will belong to that company. Overseas subsidiaries cannot form part of a 75% group and therefore Octopus Ltd could not claim relief for any of the Rubeenian subsidiary's losses.

If Octopus sells goods to the Rubeenian subsidiary at an undervalue, the Revenue may regard this as trading at artificial prices. Octopus Ltd's profits would be artificially low so, to avoid this, the Revenue could substitute an arm's length price (i.e. market value) for the purpose of establishing the profits chargeable to corporation tax.

Octopus Ltd would be unable to claim capital allowances in respect of any capital expenditure incurred by the Rubeenian subsidiary, because the assets acquired would not belong to Octopus Ltd.

Assuming that the Rubeenian subsidiary is controlled from Rubeenia, Octopus Ltd will only pay UK corporation tax on any dividends actually received from the Rubeenian subsidiary. This should result in a lower UK corporation tax charge than if the establishment were set up as a branch. The dividends would be taxable in the accounting period in which they are received. Octopus Ltd could therefore delay its UK liability by delaying the payment of dividends by the Rubeenian subsidiary.

c) i) The Rubeenian subsidiary would be classed as a controlled foreign company because it is:

- resident outside the UK
- controlled by persons resident in the UK
- subject to a lower level of taxation in the country in which it is resident (less than 75% of the corresponding UK rate).

ii) If the Inland Revenue so directs, the subsidiary's chargeable profits will be apportioned to Octopus Ltd and thus brought within the charge to UK corporation tax.

iii) This apportionment of profits can be avoided by satisfying any one of the following tests:

- the subsidiary's profits are less than £20,000 for a 12 month accounting period
- the subsidiary distributes at least 50% of its accounting profits as a dividend within 18 months of the end of its accounting period
- at least 35% of the subsidiary's ordinary share capital is held by the public and was dealt in on a recognised Stock Exchange within the accounting period
- the exempt activities test. This is satisfied if the subsidiary is not an investment company, and derives less than 50% of its gross income from connected persons
- the Inland Revenue is satisfied that the motive for setting up the subsidiary was not primarily a reduction in the liability to UK tax.

d) As Frank Squid has come to the UK to take up employment which is to last for more than two years, the extra-statutory concession applies. This means that he will be regarded as resident from the date of his arrival until the date of his departure. As he intends to remain in the UK for more than three years, he will be ordinarily resident for the same period. All of his Schedule E emoluments will therefore be assessable under case I. The fact that some of these emoluments relate to overseas duties is irrelevant.

As Frank proposes to return to Rubeenia, he will not have established a UK domicile. His overseas interest can therefore only be assessable to the extent that it is remitted to the UK. During 1994/95 he will thus be assessed on £500.

12

21 a) i) Residence is usually determined in respect of a complete fiscal year. An individual can be classed as resident if he is present in the UK for 183 days or more, or if he makes habitual and substantial visits to the UK. However, as Mark is leaving the UK in order to take up employment abroad, which will last for more than one complete fiscal year, the extra-statutory concession applies. This means that the fiscal year will be split and he will be treated as not resident and not ordinarily resident in the UK from the date of his departure until the date of his return. If his visits to the UK should increase to three months per annum, however, he would be treated as remaining resident and ordinarily resident throughout his time abroad.

ii) Liability to UK inheritance tax is determined by domicile not residence. Mark will remain domiciled in the UK as he intends to return to the UK when his contract is eventually terminated. He will therefore remain liable to UK IHT on his worldwide assets.

b) As Mark will be not resident in the UK, his overseas sources of income will not be within the scope of UK income tax. He will, however, remain liable to UK income tax on his UK sources of income.

The UK agent, who is managing the letting of Mark's property, will be responsible for deducting basic rate tax from his rental income. The tax is calculated after the deduction of any expenses, including the mortgage interest. The agent must account to the Revenue for the tax deducted.

Certain UK government securities are exempt from UK income tax if held by someone who is non-UK resident. The dividends will be received net of lower rate tax. As Mark will remain a British citizen, he will still be entitled to a personal allowance. This may enable him to claim a repayment of any UK tax suffered.

c) i) Mark will not be liable to UK CGT whilst he is not resident and not ordinarily resident. He could therefore dispose of any of his UK assets without attracting UK CGT. He should, however, delay making any disposals until 1995/96, as the Revenue have the power to refuse to grant the extra-statutory concession if they believe it is being used to avoid UK tax. He should also consider any liability to foreign CGT that he may incur.

ii) Once he returns to the UK and becomes UK resident, he will be liable to UK CGT on his worldwide assets. He should therefore dispose of any overseas assets prior to the fiscal year in which he returns to the UK.

As previously mentioned, liability to UK IHT is determined by domicile. As Mark remains UK domiciled throughout, he will remain liable to UK IHT on his worldwide assets.

d) Tabitha will not be outside the UK for a full tax year, therefore she will remain resident in the UK throughout the period of the contract. Her earnings will be assessable under Case I of Schedule E.

If Tabitha can establish a qualifying period of 365 days, her overseas earnings will qualify for a 100% deduction. Tabitha's contract covers a period of 395 days. Days spent in the UK may count towards the qualifying period provided that they satisfy two tests:

- they do not exceed 62 continuous days, and
- they do not exceed 1/6 of the qualifying period to date.

Visits to the UK in November and March would both satisfy the first test as neither visit would exceed 31 days.

The second test is performed at the start of each return to the UK:

Dates	*Overseas*	*UK*	*1/6*
1/9/94 – 31/10/94	61		
1/11/94 – 30/11/94		30	
1/12/94 – 28/2/95	90	—	
	151	30	30
1/3/95 – 31/3/95		31	
1/4/95 – 30/9/95	183	—	
	334	61	65

It will therefore be acceptable for Tabitha to return to the UK during both November 1994 and March 1995 without it affecting her entitlement to the 100% deduction. She should, however, be aware that the November visit only just satisfies the 1/6 rule and so she should be careful not to prolong it.

Any travelling and accommodation costs paid by Genie plc will be classed as assessable emoluments. Tabitha can, however, claim deductions in respect of:

- the costs of travelling to and from the UK
- travelling incurred in the performance of her duties
- board and lodgings whilst overseas.

22 a) i) The Financial Services Act 1986 requires all those involved in investment business to be authorised by either:

- a recognised professional body, such as the ACCA, or
- a self-regulating organisation, such as SFA, IMRO, LAUTRO or FIMBRA, or
- the Securities and Investment Board.

It is now a criminal offence for any person to carry on investment business without authorisation.

ii) Authorisation is needed in respect of investment activities. These fall into four categories:

- dealing in investments, including buying, selling or underwriting investments
- arranging deals in investments, apart from arranging introductions to a broker who does not act as a principal or agent
- managing investments
- giving investment advice.

Investments, for these purposes include shares, debentures, gilts, options, futures, endowment policies, etc.

iii) Certain types of investment are not covered by the definition in the Act and can therefore be undertaken without authorisation. These types of investments are:

- real property
- works of art
- gold
- building society deposits
- savings accounts
- repayment mortgages.

b) As Phoebe is a member of an occupational pension scheme, she cannot contribute to a personal pension scheme in respect of her earnings. She could, however, make Additional Voluntary Contributions (AVCs) to her employer's scheme. The

12

maximum contribution is 15% of Phoebe's gross emoluments, less any sums already contributed to her employer's scheme. AVCs are dealt with through the PAYE system in the same way as regular contributions to the scheme.

Alternatively, Phoebe could pay free-standing AVCs into a separate scheme run by an insurance company. These premiums would be paid net of basic rate tax, and the same maximum limits apply. Unlike personal pension schemes, unused relief cannot be carried forward.

c) i) The payment to Derek has been classed as an ex-gratia payment, so it would appear that he was not contractually entitled to it. If it could be proved that the payment was a reward for past services, it would be taxable in full. Assuming that this is not the case, it escapes the normal rules of Schedule E but is brought into charge by s148 ICTA 1988. The first £30,000 of such payments are tax free. Statutory redundancy payments are exempt from tax, but count as part of the non-taxable £30,000. Therefore Derek will be liable to tax on £10,000 of his £40,000 lump sum.

ii) The issue of the shares cannot be approved as a profit sharing scheme because only the directors are entitled to participate. Phoebe will therefore be assessable under Schedule E on the difference between the market value of the shares issued to her and the price she paid for them:

	£
Market value (3,000 × £4)	12,000
Cost (3,000 × £1)	(3,000)
Schedule E charge	9,000

The granting of the option does not give rise to a Schedule E charge. However, when the option is exercised, an assessable benefit will arise calculated in the same manner as above:

	£
Market value at date of exercise (assumed 5,000 × £10)	50,000
Cost (5,000 × (£4 × 70%))	(14,000)
Schedule E charge	36,000

The option does not qualify as an approved share option scheme as it is exercisable within three years of the date of its grant and the price paid is significantly less than the market value at the date of the grant.

d) i) Phoebe will be assessed under Schedule E on the benefit of the car and fuel. The car benefit is based on the list price of the car at the time it is first provided. The cost of the car will not include the mobile telephone as this is a separate benefit:

	£
Car (£18,800 × 35%)	6,580
Fuel (diesel)	580
Mobile phone (scale charge)	200
	7,360

The scale charge in respect of the mobile telephone may be reduced to nil if there is no private use.

There are no NIC implications for Phoebe in respect of the provision of either the car or the telephone.

ii) Quest plc will be able to claim capital allowances in respect of the car. These will be based on the VAT inclusive cost as the VAT is not reclaimable. The maximum writing down allowance is £3,000 per year.

The cost of fuel is a deductible expense. Quest plc can recover any input tax suffered on the fuel, but will have to account for output tax based on the Schedule E fuel scale charges. The annual charge is thus: £580 × 7/47 = £86.38. This output tax can be avoided by not reclaiming any input tax.

The input tax of £105 (£705 × 7/47) paid in respect of the mobile telephone may be reclaimed. The net cost of £800 is eligible for capital allowances of 25% p.a. calculated using the reducing balance method. The costs of telephone calls are deductible in computing profits chargeable to corporation tax. The input tax incurred on the business calls is also deductible.

Quest plc will have to pay class 1A NIC in respect of the car and fuel. The charge will be (6,580 + 580) × 10.2% = £730.32. This is deductible in computing the company's taxable profits.

SECTION

13

ANSWERS TO PILOT PAPER

This section provides advice on how to answer the pilot paper given in Section 10. You will gain the maximum benefit from this Section if you attempt the pilot paper first. Each answer gives you an idea of the approach, format and content required to obtain high marks in the examination.

1 a) i) Investment activity covers:

- dealing in investments, i.e. buying, selling, subscribing for or underwriting investments
- arranging deals in investments, i.e. making introductions to someone who deals in investments, excluding introductions to an authorised intermediary
- managing investments for a third party
- giving investment advice, such as recommending particular investments.

ii) The definition of investments covers personal equity plans and government stocks, but excludes TESSAs.

iii) Some of the investments being considered by George and Mildred fall within the definition of investments in the Financial Services Act 1986. Selecting appropriate investments falls within the definition of investment activity. None of the activities are 'excluded'. The final question is whether these activities constitute carrying on a business. Giving advice to relatives or friends who are not clients is excluded from the definition of business. George is a friend and will not be charged a fee, therefore it is probably not necessary to be authorised in order to give him advice. Mildred, however, will be charged a fee, so advice given to her will probably be classed as a business activity and the adviser must therefore be authorised.

b) i) *Personal equity plans* – individuals aged 18 and over who are resident and ordinarily resident in the UK can invest up to £6,000 in a general PEP and £3,000 in a single company PEP per year. The plan is managed by a plan manager who purchases investments and holds them on the individual's behalf. The investments must be ordinary shares of companies quoted in the UK or EC, or unit or investment trusts containing a minimum of 50% of such shares. Investment of up to £1,500 per year is permitted in non-qualifying unit or investment trusts. There is no relief for the initial investment into the plan, but dividends are free of income tax and no CGT is charged on disposals or withdrawals from the plan.

Government stocks – there is no maximum amount of investment in government stocks. Interest paid to UK residents is subject to income tax. Interest is usually paid net, apart from interest paid on War Loan or stocks purchased through the National Savings Stock Register. Where interest is paid gross, it is taxable under Schedule D case III, the tax normally being due on 1 January in the year of assessment. Where interest is paid net, any higher rate tax is collected by means of a taxed income assessment. The normal due date is 1 December following the year of assessment. Disposals are not subject to CGT, however, any accrued interest included in the disposal proceeds may be chargeable to income tax under the accrued income scheme if the securities held have a nominal value in excess of £5,000.

TESSAs – a Tax Exempt Special Savings Account may be opened with either a bank or a building society. Each individual may hold only one account, which must remain open for five years in order to retain its tax exempt status. The account may be opened with a maximum investment of £3,000 in the first year. Up to £1,800 can be invested in each subsequent year up to an overall maximum of £9,000. During the five-year term investors may only withdraw amounts equivalent to the interest credited less basic rate tax. Withdrawals in excess of this will cause the account to lose its tax exempt status and all the interest will be taxable at that date.

ii) *PEPs* – there is no minimum period of investment in a PEP and thus one would be suitable for George. Two or three years would enable the investment to show some capital growth. George would also benefit by saving income tax at 40% on the plan's income. The CGT exemption is probably of little benefit as any gains George makes may already be covered by his annual exemption. The plan could be liquidated easily without losing its tax exemptions, but George should weigh up the cost of making the investment against the tax savings involved.

As a basic rate taxpayer, a PEP is probably of less use to Mildred, although it will enable her to build up a greater investment than could otherwise be done out of taxed income. A general PEP is less risky than investing in the stock market directly as the sum invested is spread over a number of different shares.

Government stocks – these are traditionally seen as a safe investment because, although the price may fluctuate according to prevailing market rates of interest, an investor is unlikely to lose all his capital. George would be required to pay higher rate tax on his income but could avoid tax on any gains. Once again this CGT exemption is of benefit only if George currently utilises his annual exemption. There is a ready market for the stocks so George could obtain access to his capital at any time without penalty. Returns could be further safeguarded by purchasing index-linked stocks.

TESSAs – a TESSA would be most suitable for Mildred as she does not require access to her capital and there is no risk to her capital. She should, however, consider whether the return will be adequate in the light of inflation. George may consider it worthwhile investing as interest rates are frequently above those on offer to normal savings accounts. He should, however, check whether the institution imposes a penalty for the early closure of the account. He would also be required to pay higher rate tax on the total interest accrued to the date of closure.

2 a) August 1986: The transfer of £100,000 is reduced by two years annual exemptions to £94,000. This is covered by the nil rate band.

September 1991: The transfer of £90,000 is reduced by the marriage exemption of £5,000 and two years annual exemptions totalling £6,000. The IHT due is:

	Gross	*IHT*
	£	£
August 1986	94,000	–
September 1991	79,000	9,200
	173,000	9,200

$(173{,}000 - 150{,}000) \times 40\% = 9{,}200$

The IHT due is reduced by taper relief of 20% to £7,360. It is payable by Susan on 30 June 1995.

October 1991: The transfer is reduced by business property relief of 100%. There is thus no IHT due in respect of this transfer.

December 1994:	£
Estate at death	465,000
Less 50% BPR on Nobody Ltd shares	(22,500)
	442,500

On death, the August 1986 transfer falls out of the calculation as it is more than seven years before the date of death. The nil rate band is reallocated to the September 1991 transfer, leaving £71,000 (150,000 – 79,000) to set against the estate. The IHT due is therefore (442,500 – 71,000) × 40% = £148,600. It is due on 30 June 1995.

b) At present Peter's will makes no use of the exemption applying to the transfer of assets between spouses. As Peter's wife has no assets of her own, on death her nil rate band will be wasted. The will should therefore be changed to give Peter's wife at least £150,000 of his assets. If the wife were given more than £150,000 it would give scope to further reduce the overall IHT bill as she could then make use of her annual exemption.

The will could also be amended to pass assets to Peter's grandchildren. This would not save IHT immediately but may do so in the future as it would reduce the estates of Susan and Jenny.

If the will was not changed, Susan and Jenny could make the changes after Peter's death by means of a deed of family arrangement. Such a deed must be made within two years of the date of death, by the persons who were due to benefit under the will. A written election must be submitted to the Inspector of Taxes within six months of the date of the deed. The deed would not be treated as a transfer of value by Susan and Jenny as the terms of the deed would simply replace those of the will.

c) In order to claim business property relief Jenny must still own the business at the date of Peter's death. If the business is sold, Jenny will be liable to pay IHT of £51,200 (£160,000 × 40% = £64,000 less 20% tapering relief). The sale proceeds may be substituted for the value at the date of transfer as the business has fallen in value.

In addition, the IHT due on the estate will be increased by £28,400 (£71,000 × 40%) as there will be no nil rate band available.

These additional liabilities far outweigh the loss in value of the business, so the sale should be delayed until after Peter's death.

d) If quoted investments are sold within 12 months of the date of death, the estate value may be reduced by any loss on sale. All such investments sold within that twelve month period must be taken into account. If the executors sold the shares in Bluechip plc, the IHT could be reduced by £1,600 (£4,000 × 40%). However, if they also sold the shares in Giltedge plc, no reduction could be claimed as the profit on the sale of the Giltedge shares exceeds the loss on the sale of the Bluechip shares.

A reduction can also be claimed in respect of losses on land sold within four years of the date of death. If the executors sold the holiday home, the IHT could be reduced by £6,000 (£15,000 × 40%). This reduction could not be claimed if the private residence were sold within the same period, as the forecast profit exceeds the loss on the holiday home.

In deciding whether to make these sales, the executors should consider whether they will be able to utilise the resulting capital losses. It may prove more beneficial for the assets to be sold at a loss by the beneficiaries, depending on their marginal rate of tax.

3 a) As Andrew's business is commencing after 5 April 1994, he will be subject to the new current year basis of assessment. His capital allowances will be calculated in respect of his accounting periods and will be treated as trading expenses. They are thus deductible in computing his Schedule DI profits.

A depooling election should be made in respect of the equipment acquired on 1 January 1996. The capital allowances due will therefore be:

	General pool	Depooled	Total
	£	£	£
A/cs to 30/4/95			
Additions	25,000		
WDA 10/12	(5,208)		5,208
	19,792		
A/cs to 30/4/96			
Additions	15,000	8,000	
Disposals	(14,000)	–	
	20,792	8,000	
WDA	(5,198)	(2,000)	7,198
	15,594	6,000	
A/cs to 30/4/97			
WDA	(3,899)	(1,500)	5,399
WDV c/f	11,695	4,500	

Andrew's profits for Schedule DI purposes will therefore be:

		£
Period to 30/4/95	(33,000 – 5,208)	27,792
Year ended 30/4/96	(48,000 – 7,198)	40,802
Year ended 30/4/97	(36,000 – 5,399)	30,601

His Schedule DI assessments under the new current year basis of assessment will therefore be:

		£
1994/95	£27,792 × 9/10 =	25,013
1995/96	£27,792 + (40,802 × 2/12)	34,592
1996/97	A/cs to 30/4/96	40,802
1997/98	A/cs to 30/4/97	30,601

Overlap relief will be available in respect of the profits of £25,013 assessed in both 1994/95 and 1995/96 and also in respect of the profits of £6,800 assessed in both 1995/96 and 1996/97. This will be given either when the business comes to an end or in any earlier year of assessment for which the basis period is longer than twelve months.

b) If Hilda is an employee for the first accounting period, any salary paid to her (plus employers' NIC at 10.2%) will be deductible in computing the business's Schedule DI profits. The operation of the commencement rules will enable the business to obtain relief almost twice for the one year's salary paid to Hilda. However, this benefit is only temporary as it will reduce the profits eligible for overlap relief.

As an employee, Hilda will be liable under Schedule E. Income tax and class 1 NIC will be deducted under the PAYE scheme. The Inspector will need to be satisfied that any salary is justifiable in relation to the work undertaken.

If Hilda is taken on as an equal partner from 1 July 1995, the assessable profits computed above will simply be divided equally between her and Andrew. However, Hilda will be treated as commencing to trade as at this date, and this will give rise to further overlap profits. Income tax and class 4 NIC will be payable in two equal instalments: 1 January in the year of assessment and 1 July in the following year. As an equal partner, Hilda's income from the partnership will not need to be justified to the Inspector.

Overall, the new commencement rules result in little, if any, benefit compared to the alternative of bringing Hilda into partnership from the commencement of trading on 1 July 1994.

Each partner will own a fractional share of the partnership's assets. This should result in a reduction in the CGT charged on any disposals as each partner has an annual exemption. As a partner, Hilda will be able to claim retirement relief on the eventual disposal of the business. This should result in the maximum possible relief as each partner will be 55 and will have been in business for ten years.

For IHT purposes, Andrew and Hilda each have annual exemptions which can be used to reduce the value of the business when it is eventually transferred to their son. This is of little benefit if the business qualifies for 100% business property relief, but would be useful if there were non-qualifying assets.

c) At present Andrew is liable at 40% while Hilda is only liable at 25%. Any tax planning measures should therefore aim to ensure that Hilda fully utilises her basic rate band. The couple can each have income of £27,145 (3,445 + 23,700) before they start paying higher rate tax. To achieve this, the building society account could be put into joint names. The income would then automatically be split equally by the Revenue.

The unfurnished property should also be put into joint names, as this will enable the gain arising on disposal to be reduced by two annual exemptions instead of just one.

Any transfers from Andrew to Hilda will also benefit the couple's IHT position as, at present, Hilda's nil rate band is wasted whilst Andrew's estate exceeds his nil rate band.

4 a) i) This structure will not meet Magee plc's residence requirements as companies incorporated in the UK are resident in the UK for tax purposes, irrespective of where directors' meetings are held.

ii) This structure will also not meet the residence requirements as companies not incorporated in the UK are treated as UK resident for tax purposes if their central management and control are in the UK. If the directors' meetings are the forum for exercising central management and control then the fact that such meetings are held in the UK will establish a UK residence for Gavin Ltd.

iii) This structure should meet the residence requirements as it appears that the company's central management and control is exercised outside the UK.

(Note that companies which are resident in the UK, but which would be regarded as resident in another country for the purposes of a double taxation agreement, will be treated as not resident in the UK.)

b) i) A controlled foreign company (CFC) is one which is:

- ▶ resident outside the UK,
- ▶ controlled by persons resident in the UK, and
- ▶ subject to a lower level of taxation in the country in which it is resident.

A lower level of taxation means less than 75% of the corresponding rate of UK tax.

ii) Gavin Ltd falls within the definition of a CFC. The chargeable profits of a CFC are apportioned to UK resident corporate shareholders and thus brought within the scope of UK corporation tax. Magee plc's taxable profits will therefore be increased by £420,000 if the Board of Inland Revenue so directs. Credit will be given for the Ruritanian tax paid by Gavin Ltd:

	£
Tax on apportioned profit £420,000 × 33% =	138,600
Less double tax relief £450,000 × 8% =	(36,000)
Increase in UK liability	102,600

This apportionment can be avoided by Gavin Ltd paying a dividend equivalent to at least 50% of its distributable profits within 18 months of the end of its accounting period. This will affect Magee plc's UK liability as follows:

	£
Gavin's accounting profits	400,000
Less Ruritanian tax	(36,000)
Distributable profits	364,000
Minimum dividend (364,000 × 50%)	182,000
Underlying tax (36,000 × 50%)	18,000
Schedule D Case V income	200,000
UK corporation tax (200,000 × 33%)	66,000
Less double tax relief	(18,000)
Increase in UK liability	48,000

c) An absence of 14 months will involve Alex returning to the UK on 31 January 1996. His absence will not cover a complete fiscal year and he will remain resident and ordinarily resident throughout. If he can establish a qualifying period of 365 continuous days abroad, he will be able to claim a 100% deduction in respect of his earnings during this period. Days spent in the UK can be included in the qualifying period provided that they satisfy two tests, which are performed on each return to the UK. Days spent in the UK must not exceed:

- ▶ 62 consecutive days, and
- ▶ 1/6 of the total qualifying period to date.

The proposed visits of two weeks every three months would satisfy these tests, but any increased visits would not and would result in him remaining liable to UK tax.

An absence of 18 months will involve Alex returning to the UK on 31 May 1996. His absence will thus span a complete year. As he is taking up full-time employment abroad he will, by concession, be regarded as not resident and not ordinarily resident from the date of his departure until the date of his return – his earnings will therefore escape UK income tax. However, if his visits to the UK were substantial, he would retain his residence status and his earnings would remain taxable. Visits are substantial if they average three months per year. The proposed visits are acceptable but any increased visits may not be.

13

d) The reimbursements will be taxable emoluments under Schedule E as Tony's absence neither covers a full fiscal year, nor qualifies under the 365 day rule. However, as Tony will be absent from the UK for a period of 60 days or more, he will be able to claim a deduction in respect of some of the travelling costs. The eligible costs are those in respect of his wife and the child under 18. A maximum of two return visits per person per fiscal year are deductible. In addition, Tony will be able to claim a deduction in respect of his own travel expenses to take up the employment and to return to the UK on its completion.

5 a) There are two main consequences of being classed as a close company:

- ▶ Benefits provided to participators (who are not also employees or directors) are treated as distributions. Their cost is disallowed in the Schedule DI computation and the company must account for ACT on the cash equivalent of the benefit provided.
- ▶ If a loan is made to a participator the company must account for ACT. This is notional ACT; it is not deductible in computing the company's mainstream corporation tax. The ACT is repaid when the loan is repaid.

b) All five companies are associated and share the small companies upper and lower limits:

	£
Lower limit (300,000/5)	60,000
Upper limit (1,500,000/5)	300,000

Rose can transfer £800 of its current year's trading loss to Grunt. None of the other companies can claim Rose's loss as Rose is not a member of the same 75% group. Rose must continue to carry forward its losses brought forward of £2,000 and the remaining £600 of this year's loss.

Rose must also carry forward its own surplus ACT of £500. Rose presumably paid the dividend to Grunt under a group income election, so it will not have had to account for ACT. The only ACT paid will have been in respect of the dividend paid to minorities: £1,200 × 25% = £300 × 20/80 = £75. This ACT is surplus and must also be carried forward. A subsidiary cannot surrender ACT.

Shove must carry forward its capital losses of £8,000 and set them against its own future capital gains. Capital losses cannot be surrendered to other group members.

Holdings' management expenses may be surrendered under s402 to either Grunt, Shove or Pink. The aim should be to reduce each company's profits to the small companies lower limit of £60,000. Holdings should therefore surrender £2,000 to Shove and the balance of £20,000 to Pink.

Pink and Rose are in the same 75% group for CGT purposes, therefore the transfer of the office building will give rise to neither a gain nor a loss.

After taking account of each of the above points, the corporation tax liability of each group member will be:

	Holdings	*Grunt*	*Shove*	*Pink*	*Rose*
	£	£	£	£	£
Taxable profits	Nil	Nil	60,000	65,000	Nil
Tax due at 25%/33%			15,000	21,450	
Taper relief:					
(300,000 – 65,000) × 1/50				(4,700)	
			15,000	16,750	

c) i) Rose will leave the Holdings Ltd CGT group. As it received an office building by way of a no gain, no loss transfer within the preceding six years, it will be deemed to have disposed of the building and immediately reaquired it for its market value at the date of acquisition. This will generate a chargeable gain:

	£
Deemed disposal proceeds	170,000
Cost to group	(20,000)
Unindexed gain	150,000
Indexation: £20,000 × 0.461	(9,220)
Chargeable gain	140,780

$$\frac{142.9 - 97.8}{97.8} = 0.461$$

This gain will accrue at the later of:

- the beginning of the accounting period in which Rose Ltd leaves the group – 1 April 1995
- the date on which Rose Ltd acquired the building – 6 May 1994.

Thus the gain will be deemed to accrue on 1 April 1995.

Rose will be liable to tax at 33% less tapering relief. It would therefore be more beneficial for Rose to claim its entire loss of £1,400 against this gain, rather than surrendering £800 of it to Grunt. Rose's surplus ACT can be offset against the corporation tax due.

Grunt Ltd will have a chargeable gain on the disposal of its shares in Rose. As Shove has a capital loss it would be beneficial for Grunt to transfer the shares to Shove prior to their disposal. This transfer will be on a no gain, no loss basis and will enable the offset of Shove's capital losses.

As Rose will still be an associated company for part of the accounts year ended 31 March 1996, the small companies limits will still be divided by five. For future years, however, the limits will only be divided by four.

ii) Overseas dividends are not classed as franked investment income. Instead they are chargeable to tax under Schedule D Case V. The dividend received must normally be grossed up by the withholding tax suffered and credit will be given for the overseas tax suffered. As Holdings has no UK liability owing to its losses, it will be unable to claim credit relief. It should therefore claim expense relief instead. This provides some measure of relief as only the net dividend is included in the calculation of chargeable profits, but it is not as beneficial as credit relief. It would therefore be better if this investment were made by one of the other group companies (for example Pink or Shove) who could benefit from credit relief.

6 a) The failure to submit returns or to pay tax by the due date constitutes a default, which can lead to the issue of a surcharge liability notice. This is valid for a period of 12 months. A further default within the 12 month period causes the issue of a further liability notice and the imposition of a penalty. The penalty increases according to the number of defaults within the notice period. The first default surcharge is 2% of the VAT unpaid. The surcharge increases to 5% for the second default and by a further 5% for each subsequent default up to a maximum of 15%.

Assuming that the default in 1993 caused the issue of a surcharge liability notice, and the default in 1994 caused its extension, the 1995 default will result in the extension of the notice until 31 January 1996. As this is the second default within the notice period, a penalty of £550 (£11,000 × 5%) will be due. Default interest may also be due from the due date of 28 February 1995 until the date of payment.

AKF should ensure that sufficient staff are employed to cope with this quarter's return. Alternatively, the company could request a change to its return periods so that they correspond with its accounting period.

b) Land never qualifies for capital allowances. The two general offices and the architects and legal fees will also not qualify as the shop does not qualify as an industrial building and is not in an enterprise zone.

The Finance Act 1994 sets out a table of expenditure to help identify which items are regarded as part of a building (and thus ineligible for capital allowances) and which will qualify as plant and machinery. Items which have been specifically granted qualifying status as a result of a court decision will not lose that status. The general electrical wiring and lighting and the false ceiling will not qualify as they are regarded as part of the cost of the building (*Wimpey International* v *Warland*), whereas the lighting for displays and shop fronts will qualify as it is regarded as specialised (*Cole Bros* v *Phillips*).

Certain safety expenditure is specifically treated as plant for capital allowance purposes.

The total qualifying expenditure is therefore:

	£
Central heating and related plumbing	21,800
Ventilation system	15,100
Fire alarm and sprinkler system	13,100
Additional fire work	5,800
Lighting for displays	4,300
Shop counters	12,900
	73,000

c) The gain on the disposal of the first shop is:

	£	£
Disposal proceeds		150,000
Cost	62,000	
Enhancement expenditure	25,000	(87,000)
Unindexed gain		63,000
Indexation:		
£62,000 × 0.450	27,900	
£25,000 × 0.109	2,725	(30,625)
Chargeable gain		32,375

The base cost of the land disposed of in May 1989 was £28,333 (85,000 × 30,000/[30,000 + 60,000]). Therefore the base cost of the second shop itself is £56,667 (85,000 – 28,333). The gain on the disposal of the second shop is therefore:

	£	£
Disposal proceeds		175,000
Cost	56,667	
Less rolled over gain	(28,000)	(28,667)
Unindexed gain		146,333
Indexation: £28,667 × 0.282		(8,084)
Chargeable gain		138,249

The entire disposal proceeds are to be reinvested in the new shop therefore the gains can be rolled over, with the exception of the gain relating to the letting. £4,856 (32,375 × 15%) therefore remains chargeable.

d) i) The interest payable on the bank loan will be deductible in computing the company's Schedule DI profits. The interest will be paid gross. Any excess interest will generate a loss. The company will have no control over the amount of interest payable. The effect on the company's level of gearing should also be considered.

ii) The company has control over the amount of dividends it wishes to pay, but dividends are not deductible in computing taxable profits. Instead, they are paid out of taxed income. If AKF Ltd is unable to offset the ACT payable, this will effectively increase the cost of paying the dividends. Any surplus ACT can be carried forward indefinitely. If the new issue is to be made to minorities, this will result in a dilution of Abdul's control. The effect on the company's earnings per share figure should also be considered.

e) i) The profit related pay scheme (PRP) allows employees to receive a certain amount of pay free of income tax, but not national insurance. The company makes a contribution to the scheme based on a percentage of the profits of an employment unit over a 12 month period. This contribution is distributed to eligible employees as profit related pay (PRP).

ii) At least 80% of the eligible employees in an employment unit must be included in the scheme. However, part-timers (working less than 20 hours per week) and employees with less than three years' service may be excluded.

iii) Abdul himself could not benefit under the scheme as it is not open to employees who, together with associates, hold more than 25% of the company's ordinary share capital.

iv) There are a number of conditions which must be met in order to obtain Inland Revenue approval:

- The scheme must have written rules setting out the way in which the company's contribution will be calculated and how it is to be distributed.
- PRP is limited to the lower of £4,000 or 20% of total pay per profit making year.
- The employment unit can be the whole or part of the business.
- The profit must be calculated consistently from year to year and must be audited by an independent accountant.

SECTION

14

ANSWERS TO MOCK EXAMINATION

This Section enables you to judge how well you fared in the mock examination given in Section 11. Don't forget, to gain maximum benefit from this Section, you should attempt the mock examination under exam conditions first.

1 a) As profits are rising, the Inland Revenue will elect under s63 for the penultimate and antepenultimate years' assessments to be revised to actual figures:

		£
1994/95	(51,000 × 2/12) + 28,000	36,500
1993/94	(48,000 × 2/12) + (51,000 × 10/12)	50,500
1992/93	(45,000 × 2/12) + (48,000 × 10/12)	47,500
1991/92	PYB accounts to 31/5/90	35,000

The capital allowance basis periods are:

1994/95	6/4/94 – 30/11/94
1993/94	6/4/93 – 5/4/94
1992/93	1/6/90 – 5/4/93
1991/92	1/6/89 – 31/5/90

As Abigail controls Abigail Ltd, the two parties are connected. The assets are deemed to be disposed of at their market values, thus giving rise to an overall balancing charge. In order to avoid this balancing charge, both parties can elect for the assets to be transferred at their written down values. This election must be made in writing within two years of the date of the transfer. Assuming that the election is made, the capital allowances will be as follows:

	General pool	*Car 1*	*Car 2*	*Less PU*	*Total*
1991/92	£	£	£	£	£
WDV b/f	16,000	7,800			
WDA	(4,000)	(1,950)		780	5,170
	12,000	5,850			
1992/93					
Additions	8,600				
	20,600	5,850			
WDA	(5,150)	(1,463)		585	6,028
	15,450	4,387			
1993/94					
Additions			15,000		
Disposals		(2,000)			
	15,450	2,387	15,000		
B/A		(2,387)		955	1,432
WDA	(3,863)		(3,000)	1,200	5,663
	11,587	–	12,000		7,095

1994/95				
WDA × 8/12	(1,931)	(2,000)	800	3,131
	9,656	10,000		
Disposal	(9,656)	(10,000)		
	–	–		

The net Schedule DI assessments are therefore:

	1991/92	*1992/93*	*1993/94*	*1994/95*
	£	£	£	£
Schedule DI	35,000	47,500	50,500	36,500
Capital allowances	(5,170)	(6,028)	(7,095)	(3,131)
	29,830	41,472	43,405	33,369

b) The goodwill had no cost and can therefore have no indexation. Its disposal will give rise to a capital gain of £50,000.

The plant, motor car and net current assets are not chargeable to CGT.

The gain arising on the disposal of the freehold premises is:

	£
Sale proceeds	95,000
Cost	(45,000)
Unindexed gain	50,000
Indexation: £45,000 × 0.618	(27,810)
Chargeable gain	22,190

If Abigail receives shares as consideration for the disposal, the full gain will automatically be held over against the base cost of the shares. Assuming that Abigail has no other gains in 1994/95, her annual exemption will be wasted. She should therefore take part of the consideration in the form of cash in order to generate a chargeable gain of £5,800. The total consideration is £205,000. Of this, £16,470 (205,000 × 5,800/72,190) should be in cash, with the balance in shares.

c) Abigail will be required to deregister within 30 days of the cessation of her business. No output tax is chargeable as the business is transferred as a going concern.

Abigail Ltd must register within 30 days of its trade commencing. As Abigail was registered for VAT, her turnover is taken into account in determining when Abigail Ltd is required to register.

It is possible for Abigail Ltd to take over Abigail's registration number, however this will involve taking responsibility for Abigail's debts.

d) If the business goes into liquidation, Abigail's father will have a capital loss calculated in the usual way. This capital loss may be set off against capital gains in the same or future years.

As Abigail's father subscribed for the shares and because Abigail Ltd is an unquoted trading company, he can claim relief under s574 ICTA 1988. This enables him to set the loss against his statutory total income of the year of the loss and/or the following year. This claim requires an election within two years of the end of the year for which the loss is claimed.

2 a) i) The chargeable gain arising if the gift of shares is made by Richard is:

1985 Pool	*Number*	*Cost*
	£	£
August 1986	8,000	30,000
Indexation to May 1990:		
£30,000 × $\frac{126.2 - 97.8}{97.8}$		8,712
Rights issue (1 for 4)	2,000	10,000
	10,000	48,712
Indexation to December 1994:		
£48,712 × $\frac{144.0 - 126.2}{126.2}$		6,871
	10,000	55,583

For CGT purposes the shares in Morning Ltd are valued at £8 each, since the gift of 20,000 shares represents a 20% shareholding.

Disposal proceeds (10,000 at £8)	80,000
Indexed cost	(55,583)
Chargeable gain	24,417

1982 Pool

	Number	*Cost*	*1982 Value*
		£	£
July 1977	24,000	24,000	48,000
Rights issue (1 for 4)	6,000	30,000	30,000
	30,000	54,000	78,000
Disposal (1/3)	(10,000)	(18,000)	(26,000)
Remaining in pool	20,000	36,000	52,000
Disposal proceeds (10,000 at £8)		80,000	80,000
Cost/1982 value		(18,000)	(26,000)
Unindexed gain		62,000	54,000
Indexation:			
£48,000 × 1/3 × 0.814		(13,024)	(13,024)
£30,000 × 1/3 × 0.141		(1,410)	(1,410)
Chargeable gain		47,566	39,566

The lower gain of £39,566 is taken. Richard's total chargeable gain is therefore £63,983 (24,417 + 39,566).

ii) The chargeable gain arising if the gift of shares is made by Judy is:

1985 Pool	*Number*	*Cost*
	£	£
September 1989	20,000	90,000
Indexation to May 1990:		
£90,000 × $\frac{126.2 - 116.6}{116.6}$		7,410
	20,000	97,410
Proceeds from sale of rights		(1,200)
	20,000	96,210

Indexation to December 1994:

$£96,210 \times \frac{144.0 - 126.2}{126.2}$		13,570
	20,000	109,780

Disposal proceeds (20,000 at £8)	160,000
Indexed cost	(109,780)
Chargeable gain	50,220

Judy's sale of her rights for £1,200 is less than 5% (20,000 at £5 × 5% = £5,000) of the value of her shareholding at that date, and so is simply deducted from her base cost.

As Morning Ltd is an unquoted trading company, holdover relief may be claimed irrespective of whether it is Richard or Judy who makes the gift.

b) i) The Inheritance Tax liability is computed using the related property provisions as these result in a higher value transferred as compared to the unrelated valuation. Prior to the disposal, Richard held 40% of the shares in Morning Ltd. Judy held 20%, which gave the couple a combined holding of 60%. After the disposal, the couple will have a combined holding of 40%.

The value of the transfer if Richard makes the gift is:

	£
Before transfer: 40,000 × £17 =	680,000
After transfer: 20,000 × £12 =	240,000
Value transferred	440,000

ii) The value of the transfer if Judy makes the gift is:

	£
Before transfer: 20,000 × £17 =	340,000
After transfer:	–
Value transferred	340,000

No IHT is due at the time of making the gift as it is a PET. Liability can only arise if the donor were to die within seven years of making the gift. As the property transferred was part of a holding of more than 25% in an unquoted company, which was owned by the transferor for over two years prior to the date of transfer, it qualifies for business property relief at 100%. This relief will continue to be available provided that Anthony owns the shares from the date of the transfer until the date of the donor's death, or Anthony's death if earlier.

3 a) i) An accounting period commences when a company first comes within the charge to corporation tax by carrying on a business or by acquiring a source of income. In Minders Ltd's case, it is debatable when the accounting period commences. It could arguably commence on 1 June 1994 when the company started purchasing cars for resale. Alternatively, it could commence on 1 July 1994 when the business made its first sale.

An accounting period finishes twelve months after it commences, or at the end of the company's period of account. In Minders Ltd's case, the accounting period will end on 31 March 1995 as this is the company's accounting date.

ii) For corporation tax purposes, the advertising and refurbishment expenditure are classed as pre-trading expenditure. As the expenditure was incurred

14

within seven years of the commencement of trade, it will be treated as if incurred on the first day of trading. Assuming that the expenditure is classed as revenue, it will thus be deductible in computing the schedule DI profits for the period to 31 March 1995.

The state of the building at the date of purchase must be considered when determining whether the refurbishment expenditure is deductible. If the building was not usable, the expenditure will be classed as capital and disallowed under the Law Shipping principle. If the building was usable the expenditure will be allowable following the Odeon Associated Theatres case.

For VAT purposes, no distinction is made between capital and revenue expenditure. All of the input tax suffered will be deductible as the services were supplied within six months of the company registering for VAT.

b) Under the second-hand goods scheme, the company will account for VAT on its profit margin rather than on the selling price of the goods. The amount of output tax due will be calculated using the formula: profit margin × 7/47. The output tax will be due in respect of the period in which the goods are sold. Input tax cannot be reclaimed on goods purchased for resale under this scheme, but can be reclaimed as normal in respect of expenditure.

A comprehensive stock record system must be maintained as a condition of using the second-hand goods scheme, so that the profit margin on each car sold may be easily identified.

c) A distinction is drawn between the provision of a car to Arthur, who is a director, and to Terry who is not.

For Minders Ltd, the cost of purchasing the car for Arthur is eligible for capital allowances. The allowances are calculated on the VAT inclusive cost, as input tax suffered on the purchase of cars is not deductible. The allowances will be time-apportioned in this first accounting period as it does not cover a full twelve months. The running costs of this car are deductible in computing the company's schedule DI profits.

Arthur will be assessed under Schedule E. His benefit will be reduced by one-third as his business mileage equates to over 2,500 p.a. The charge will thus be: (£11,000 × 35%) × 2/3 = £2,567.

Minders Ltd will be required to account for class 1A NIC on the provision of the car to Arthur. The amount will be based on the Schedule E benefit charge of £2,567, so the NIC due will be £261.83 (£2,567 × 10.2%). This amount will also be deductible in computing the company's Schedule DI profits.

The provision of the car to Terry will be classed as a distribution, and Minders Ltd will be required to account for ACT. The amount of the distribution is equivalent to the Schedule E charge (£14,000 × 35% = £4,900) so the ACT due is £1,225 (£4,900 × 20/80). Capital allowances will not be available in respect of this car.

Terry is not an employee and cannot be assessed under Schedule E. Instead, he is treated as being in receipt of Schedule F income of £6,125 (4,900 × 100/80). He will have a tax credit of £1,225 (6,125 × 20%) to offset against his income tax liability.

d) Minders Ltd must account for ACT of £7,750 (£31,000 × 20/80) on the loan. This is notional ACT; it is not paid under the quarterly accounting system and is not deductible in computing the company's mainstream corporation tax liability. It must be paid within 14 days of the end of the accounting period in which the loan is made, and will be repaid when the loan is repaid.

There are no income tax implications for Terry, unless the loan is written off. In that event, the amount released is treated as if it were a dividend received by him. It is thus grossed up by the lower rate of income tax and treated as Terry's income. If Terry is a lower or basic rate taxpayer, there will be no further tax to pay. If he is a higher rate taxpayer, he will have to pay an additional 20% tax on this income (40% – 20%).

4 a) Priam would have acquired a domicile of origin at birth. This would have been the domicile of his father, assuming his parents were married. The actual country of birth is irrelevant. Until the age of 16, Priam would have had a domicile of dependency; his domicile would follow that of his father. After the age of 16, Priam could acquire a domicile of choice. In order to change your domicile it is necessary to take up residence in a country with the intention of making that country your permanent home.

For IHT purposes, Priam could be deemed domiciled in the UK if he had been resident in the UK for 17 out of the preceding 20 years of assessment, ending with the year of assessment in which a chargeable transfer occurs.

b) The location of assets for IHT purposes, depends on the type of asset under consideration:

- Tangible property is located wherever it is physically situated. The main residence and the jewellery are located in the UK, whereas the Wantai residence and the antiques are situated in Wantai.
- Shares and securities are located in the country in which they are registered, or in which they are normally dealt. The Wantan Inc shares and government stocks are situated in Wantai, whereas the UK government stocks are situated in the UK.
- Debts are located in the country in which the debtor is resident. The loan to Priam's brother is situated in Wantai. The use to which the loan was put is irrelevant.
- Bank accounts are located wherever the branch is. The bank deposits of £28,000 are situated in the UK despite the fact that the money is held by the Wantai Bank.

c) i) If Priam were not UK domiciled at the time of his death, only his UK property would be chargeable to IHT:

	£
Personalty:	
Jewellery	25,000
Bank deposits	28,000
Government stocks: 15,000 × 99p	14,850
	67,850
Realty:	
Main residence	95,000
	162,850
Less nil rate band	(150,000)
Chargeable at 40%	12,850
Tax due: £12,850 × 40% =	5,140

The gambling debts have not been deducted as they are not imposed by law and were also presumably not incurred for full and valuable consideration.

ii) If Priam were UK domiciled at the date of his death, he would be liable to UK IHT on his worldwide property. This would increase his IHT as follows:

	£	£
Estate (as before)		162,850
Wantai residence	45,000	
Wantan Inc: 20,000 × 304p	60,800	
Antiques	30,000	
Loan	16,000	
Wantai stocks	19,000	170,800
		333,650
Less nil rate band		(150,000)
Chargeable at 40%		183,650
Tax due: £183,650 × 40% =		73,460
Less double tax relief		(37,605)
IHT due		35,855

Double tax relief is the lower of:

1) The overseas tax suffered	50,000
2) The UK tax due on the overseas assets: £170,800 × 22.017% =	37,605

The UK tax due on the overseas assets has been calculated using the estate rate which is computed as follows:

73,460/333,650 × 100 = 22.017%

5 BLACKWELLS PLC

The tax implications of the purchase of Brownleys Ltd

a) *The proposed treatment of Brownleys Ltd*

i) Brownleys Ltd currently has unutilised trading losses which can only be carried forward under s393(1) against its future profits of the same trade. If a major change in the nature or conduct of Brownleys' trade occurs within three years of the takeover by Blackwells plc, s768 ICTA 1988 prevents the carry forward of these losses after the date of the takeover. The sale of the unprofitable premises will probably not be treated as a major change, whereas a change in the type of goods sold, or the customers or markets would be.

ii) Losses incurred after the takeover could be surrendered to other members of Blackwells plc's 75% group under s402.

iii) Brownleys Ltd cannot surrender its surplus ACT, it can only carry it forward against its own future corporation tax liabilities. Carrying forward beyond the date of the takeover will also be prevented if a major change in the nature or conduct of the trade occurs within three years of the date of the takeover.

iv) In view of the restrictions on the set off of the losses and ACT brought forward, it would be beneficial for Bownleys Ltd to continue to trade until these have been fully utilised.

b) *The proposed treatment of Brownleys' premises*

i) Premises transferred to other members of Blackwell plc's CGT group will give rise to neither a gain nor a loss. A subsidiary is a member of the CGT group if it is a 75% subsidiary of Blackwell plc. Subsubsidiaries of Blackwell plc may also be group members provided that Blackwell plc has an effective interest of over 50%. Gains can therefore be deferred until the properties are disposed of outside the group. Alternatively, if a company leaves the group within six years of receiving an asset, it will be deemed to have disposed of the asset and immediately reacquired it at its market value at the date of the transfer. The resulting gain will be treated as arising at the beginning of the accounting period in which the company leaves the group, or, if later, the date on which the asset was actually acquired from the group member.

ii) Premises transferred to non-group members will give rise to a capital gain calculated in the usual way. The premises will be deemed to be transferred at their market values as companies under common control are connected persons.

iii) Corporation tax liability could be minimised by utilising Brownleys' surplus ACT. This could be achieved by realising the capital gains in the hands of Brownleys Ltd.

iv) Capital losses cannot be transferred between group members. The premises should therefore be transferred, prior to their disposal, to any company holding capital losses. The set off of losses arising to companies joining a group is restricted. Thus the losses arising to Whiteleys Ltd may only be set off against (a) gains on assets held by Whiteleys Ltd at the date of its entry into the Blackwells plc group, or (b) gains on assets acquired by Whiteleys Ltd from outside the group and used in a trade carried on by Whiteleys Ltd before it joined the group.

c) *The purchase of new freehold and leasehold premises by other group companies*

i) All members of Blackwells' CGT group are treated as one for the purpose of making rollover relief claims. Thus if the disposal proceeds of the premises are reinvested by another group company, a rollover relief claim can be made. Any disposal proceeds not reinvested will remain chargeable.

ii) In order to claim rollover relief, the disposal proceeds must be reinvested within a period beginning one year before and ending three years after the date of disposal.

iii) If the proceeds are reinvested in a freehold property, the gain rolled over will be deducted from the base cost of the property acquired. This defers any CGT until the new property is eventually disposed of.

iv) If the proceeds are reinvested in leasehold property, the taxation treatment is different because leasehold properties are classed as depreciating assets. The gain is held over until the earliest of (a) the date the property is disposed of, (b) the date the property ceases to be used for the purpose of the trade, or (c) 10 years from the date of the acquisition of the replacement property.

v) Assuming that the new premises are intended to be retained in excess of ten years, it would be most beneficial for any gains to be held over against the cost of freehold properties as this would defer liability for the longest possible period.

vi) Industrial buildings allowance is not available in respect of the cost of the premises, unless they are situated in enterprise zones.

6 a) A distinction is made between a contract *of* service (employment) and a contract *for* services (self-employment). In determining which of these applies, a number of points will be considered:

i) *Control* Jason will be told when, where and how to perform his role. This is evidence of employment. On the other hand, he will presumably have some artistic input, which may indicate self-employment.

14

ii) *Mutual obligations* Do the producers have an obligation to provide work for Jason, and does Jason have an obligation to accept it? The producers are not obliged to provide Jason with more work when his contract comes to an end. This may be evidence of self-employment. Jason is, however, obliged to undertake any promotional work required. This is evidence of employment.

iii) *Economic reality* The fact that Jason has previously performed this type of work on a self-employed basis, may be evidence of a contract for services. However, he is not able to delegate his work and seems to bear no financial risk for the success of the show. These factors are evidence of employment.

iv) *Integration* Is Jason providing the services as an integral part of the producers' business? The Inland Revenue would consider whether other dancers are classed as employees. They would also take into account whether Jason is entitled to sick pay or holiday pay.

Jason's position is not clear-cut but, on balance, he would appear to be employed under a contract of service. He will have only one contract, which will prevent him from working for anyone else and which specifies set hours and dates of work.

Note: marks will also be available for quoting relevant case law, particularly *Fall* v *Hitchen* which found a ballet dancer to be employed under a contract of service.

b) As a self-employed taxpayer, earning £30,000 p.a., Jason's 1994/95 income tax and national insurance liabilities would be as follows:

		£
Schedule D		30,000
Less 50% class 4 NIC		(579)
		29,421
Personal allowance		(3,445)
Taxable income		25,976
Income tax due:	3,000 × 20%	600
	20,700 × 25%	5,175
	2,276 × 40%	910
		6,685
Class 2 NIC: £5.65 × 52		294
Maximum Class 4 NIC:		
(22,360 – 6,490) × 7.3%		1,158
Total liability		8,137

Jason's post tax income will therefore be £21,863 (30,000 – 8,137).

If Jason becomes an employee, he will be liable to pay the maximum class 1 NIC. This, in addition to the income tax due, will give him the following liability:

		£
Schedule E		35,000
Personal allowance		(3,445)
Taxable income		31,555
Income tax due:	3,000 × 20%	600
	20,700 × 25%	5,175
	7,855 × 40%	3,142
		8,917

Maximum class 1 NIC:

£57 × 52 × 2%	59
(430 – 57) × 52 × 10%	1,940
	10,916

The extra £5,000 offered by the London contract more than compensates for the extra income tax and NIC liabilities incurred by Jason as an employee. His post tax income will be £24,084 (35,000 – 10,916) if he accepts the contract, which makes him better off by £2,221 (24,084 – 21,863). He will, however, suffer a cash flow disadvantage because his liabilities will be met through the PAYE scheme, rather than being paid in arrears.

c) i) Jason can contribute a maximum of 17.5% of his net relevant earnings into a personal pension scheme. If he accepts the new contract, he may contribute £6,125 (35,000 × 17.5%) in respect of these earnings. As he has not previously made provision for a pension, he may utilise his unused relief for earlier years, which totals: £30,000 × 5 years × 17.5% = £26,250. Contributions are deductible in computing statutory total income. In Jason's case, relief should eliminate his higher rate liability.

If classified as an employee, pension contributions will be paid net of basic rate tax. Jason should be advised to relate back part of his premium to 1993/94 as this will enable him to reduce his higher rate liability for that year. Any premium which is to be related back should be paid by 5 April 1995 and the necessary election should be made by 5 July 1995.

The pension fund itself is free of both income tax and capital gains tax, but any pension received is subject to income tax. It is normally not possible to take a pension until the age of 50, so this is not a liquid investment. However, the Inland Revenue do permit certain professions to start to draw a pension at a much earlier age. This special treatment almost certainly applies to dancers, but it does mean that the fund will not have as long to grow and therefore any pension will be much smaller than one drawn at the age of 50.

Provided that the contract is made with a reputable company, this is a very safe and tax efficient form of investment.

ii) Jason could invest up to £6,000 per fiscal year in a general PEP and/or up to £3,000 per fiscal year in a single company PEP. It is not possible to make contributions in respect of earlier years.

No tax relief is given for the initial investment, but income and gains within the fund are free of both income tax and capital gains tax. Jason could, if he wished, arrange for any dividends to be paid to him (free of tax) rather than reinvested in the plan. There is no minimum period of time for the funds to be retained within the plan, although the longer the funds are invested, the greater the opportunity for capital growth. Jason could therefore gain easy access to his investment in an emergency. Any withdrawals from the plan are free of capital gains tax.

As the plan involves investing in equities, it obviously carries more risk than depositing money in a bank or building society. However, it also provides scope for capital growth. If a general PEP is chosen, the risk to capital will be reduced as the plan manager will spread the investment over a number of different companies.

iii) There are two types of life assurance policy; *qualifying* and *non-qualifying*. A qualifying policy is for a term of at least ten years. Premiums must be paid annually, or at shorter intervals. The proceeds paid out on maturity will be free of both income and capital gains tax.

14

For non-qualifying policies, any gain on maturity may attract liability to income tax at the difference between the higher and basic rates.

There are no limits on the amounts that may be invested in life assurance policies. The policies are liquid in the sense that they could be cashed in at any time. However, it is advisable that any policy should be allowed to run its full-term as there are usually penalties for early encashment and the investor may recover less than the capital invested.

The life assurance company will probably spread the fund over a variety of investments; e.g., shares, gilts and deposit accounts. This ensures that the risk attaching to one particular type of investment is minimised. Most funds guarantee a minimum payout, which usually means that most of the capital invested is safeguarded, but the final return is never guaranteed.

Revision Text Evaluation Form–2nd Edition

At CAEP we are interested in knowing what you think of our products and services. We would appreciate it if you could spend five minutes completing the following questionnaire.

1 From which revision text did you obtain this form?
(Please circle appropriate number)

Paper	**1**	**2**	**3**	**4**	**5**	**6**	**7**
	8	**9**	**10**	**11**	**12**	**13**	**14**

2 Did you obtain this book through: an order form in *Students' Newsletter* ☐
a bookshop ☐ other ______________

3 Did you buy this text because it was: recommended by your lecturer ☐
published by the ACCA ☐
value for money ☐
other ______________

4 Your general comments and suggestions:

____

____

____

____

____

____

____

5 About you

Are you: **a student** ☐ **a lecturer** ☐

Are you studying at a college? (Please specify) ______________

Are you resident in: **UK** ☐ **EC** ☐ **Africa** ☐ **SE Asia** ☐ **Carribean** ☐

Other ______________

Thank you for your help.

Please return your completed questionnaire using the Freepost envelope overleaf.

If you have not used the ACCA Textbook or Open Learning package for this Paper or other Papers you are studying, you may wish to do so. Copies of the Textbooks can be purchased from most good academic bookshops. Both Textbooks and Open Learning packages can also be ordered via the credit card hotline: **041-309-3999 or** *by post to:* **CAEP, PO Box 66, Glasgow G41 1BS.**

Current prices:

Textbooks:	£15.95 (per Foundation Stage Paper) £17.95 (Certificate Stage) £18.95 (Professional Stage).
Open Learning:	£95 (per Foundation Stage Paper) £100 (Certificate Stage) £115 (Professional Stage).

Postage:
Textbooks: UK £3.50 for first book, £2 each extra book; Europe and ROI £5 first, £4 each extra; Rest of the World £7.50 first, £5 each extra.
Open Learning packages prices include postage within the UK; £20 per package should be added for all other orders.
In case of difficulty or for further information please ring CAEP Customer Service on 071-396 5861/5866/5867 or Fax 071-396-5870.

Please detach here

1st fold

4th Fold

2

Customer Services
Certified Accountants Educational Projects Ltd
FREEPOST
29 Lincoln's Inn Fields
London
WC2A 3BR

3rd fold

2nd fold

Please detach here

ACCA Textbooks—Open Learning—Revision

ORDER FORM **Please indicate month and year of exam diet you are sitting e.g. 12/94, 6/95 etc.**

STAGE	MODULE	PAPER		EXAM DIET	TEXTBOOKS Product	No	Price	Charge	OPEN LEARNING PACKAGES Product	No	Price	Charge	REVISION TEXTS Product	No	Price	Charge
Foundation	A	1	Accounting Framework		T01		15.95		L01		95.00		R01		9.95	
		2	Legal Framework		T02		15.95		L02		95.00		R02		9.95	
	B	3	Management Information		T03		15.95		L03		95.00		R03		9.95	
		4	Organisational Framework		T04		15.95		L04		95.00		R04		9.95	
Certificate	C	5	Information Analysis		T05		17.95		L05		100.00		R05		9.95	
		6	Audit Framework		T06		17.95		L06		100.00		R06		9.95	
	D	7	Tax Framework		T07		17.95		L07		100.00		R07		9.95	
		8	Managerial Finance		T08		17.95		L08		100.00		R08		9.95	
Professional	E	9	Information for Control and Decision Making		T09		18.95		L09		115.00		R09		9.95	
		10	Accounting and Audit Practice		T10		18.95		L10		115.00		R10		9.95	
		11	Tax Planning		T11		18.95		L11		115.00		R11		9.95	
	F	12	Management and Strategy		T12		18.95		L12		115.00		R12		9.95	
		13	Financial Reporting Environment		T13		18.95		L13		115.00		R13		9.95	
		14	Financial Strategy		T14		18.95		L14		115.00		R14		9.95	
							Sub Total £				Sub Total £				Sub Total £	
							Postage £				Postage £				Postage £	
							Total £				Total £				Total £	
															GRAND TOTAL £	

Postage UK: Textbooks: add £3.50 for first book, plus £2 for each extra:
Revision: £2 for first, £1 for each extra: **Open Learning:** £5 for first package, £3.50 for each extra:
Europe (inc ROI): Textbooks: £5 for first, £4 for each extra: **Revision:** £3 for first, £1.50 for each extra:
Open Learning: £20 per package. **Rest of the World: Textbooks: (airmail):** £7.50 for first, £5 for each extra:
Revision: £5.50 for first, £2.50 each extra: **Open Learning:** £20 per package.
Prices are subject to change and may vary following any new VAT legislation.

Students Registration No. ______

Access/Mastercard/Visa/Switch Account Number ______

Switchcard Version No. ______ Expiry Date ______

CUSTOMER DETAILS

Order Ref. ______

Name ______

Invoice Address ______

______ Post Code ______

Country ______ Telephone ______

VAT No (Only if a firm or personally registered) ______

Delivery Address ______
(if different) ______

______ Post Code ______

Country ______ Telephone ______

ORDER TAKEN BY ______ Date ______

Please send to CAEP Ltd. PO Box 66 Glasgow G41 1BS or Fax to 041 309 3998 Credit Card Hotline: 041 309 3999

RT2-OF-94A